Seek Your Peak to Find Your Spark

April M. Williams Productions
1st Edition

Copyright © 2014 AMW, INC. All rights reserved.

All rights reserved. This book or any portion thereof may not be reproduced or used in any manner whatsoever without the express written permission of the publisher except for the use of brief quotations in a book review.

Published in the United States of America

Published by AMW Inc.

Algonquin, IL 60102

www.CyberLifeTutors.com

Electronic ISBN NOOK KINDLE, PDF 978-0-9841807-5-2

Print ISBN 978-0-9841807-6-9

Table of Contents

To Advise	7
A Life of Passion(s)	15
Adventures of the Not-So-Stay-at-Home Mom	23
A Dream Delayed is Not a Dream Denied	31
Learning to Unlearn	39
Mission to Passion	45
It is Never Too Late To Know What You Want To Do When You Grow Up	54
Hearts for Haiti	62
Importance of Understanding Your Passion and How to Find Your Passion	71
It's Never Too Late!	78
A Passion for Flight	84
Finding Passion Amidst Tragedy	90
Tails of My Life	95
Your Passion Can Adapt To Change, Just As You Do	101
Style Your Home, Style Your Life	109
Say Yes, With Enthusiasm	114
Determination: Friend or Foe?	117
Unfamiliar Territory	126
Pearl: Her Perfectly Imperfect Life Ignites My Passion	130
Dove	134
Doing the Right Thing	141
The Call	144
A Balloon Lady's Guide to a Passionate Life	150
Using Social Networking to Save Lives	158
Be a Firefly	162
My Challenge to You	167
Reviews	168
Other Works by April M. Williams	169

Acknowledgements

This book would not have been possible without the amazing people who shared their stories with me. I am honored to bring the second volume of these works to you.

Thanks Lou Camp and Mark Simon as beta readers. Cover art by April M. Williams with photograph by Rich Legg.

My deepest gratitude to my husband and best friend Noel F. Williams for his support, guidance and encouragement. We make a marvelous team.

AMW

Introduction

After publishing the first volume of this series, additional captivating stories appeared before me. I decided to publish a second volume of these works that you are now reading.

I hope you enjoy reading this anthology as much as I enjoyed meeting these authors and publishing the book.

Best, April M. Williams

President, CyberLife Tutors

To Advise

By Matt Hader

I recently came to the unnerving realization that I'm not the brightest pup in the Hader-family bunch. I'm a little slow on the uptake sometimes. 'Situationally unaware' some would say. Ask my wife. It took me several years before even realizing that I had a passion – for anything. I just knew that deep down inside I enjoyed the newly recognized activity to no end. The danger signs that this 'certain something' was a bigger part of my life than I wanted to admit to were there. They were staring me directly in the ego – with a side-glance to my cynical id.

My passion slowly blossomed from the long phone conversations, extended one-on-one lunches spent surfing the cracked leather benches in darkly lit booths of not-quite-A-rated diners. The constant emails that were exchanged. Oh, the emails. My passion grew from the time spent not acting on the actual work that I was supposed to be doing.

Just yesterday, my wife and I were spending a lovely day strolling along Michigan Avenue in downtown Chicago. She wanted to take a bit more time perusing the wares at Filene's Basement – me, not so much. So I took up temporary residence on the chairs lined up on the west side of the Chicago Water Tower. The actual Water Tower, not the eponymously named eight levels of upscale shops stacked one on top of the next located across the street. Shortly after staking my claim in the shade, I happened to strike up a conversation with a fellow male traveler running the same I-ain't-shopping-either scam on his better half. The conversation led from one thing to another, and well, he mentioned that his wife was a writer. Check that, a frustrated writer-wannabe.

Within seconds I was plying my passion.

I may need rehab.

At least now I'm finally able to step out of the denial closet and open my eyes to the truth. Which is...

From a creative point of view, I cannot stop mentoring/assisting/egging on/instructing/coaching/badgering other writers. I cannot stop from reading their work. Discussing story options, characters, word and page counts. I. Can. Not. Stop.

I didn't really mean for all of this to happen, but it happened.

It started with one person, as you'd assume, and then, over the years, one person became five. Five became 10. The first person I mentored was from my general geographic area, but over time, some of those whom I met with were from different countries. My unintended passion is now running an intercontinental course, it seems.

It started innocuously enough, as most passions do. Or addictions. I had a modicum of success a few years after starting my career, and secured an option deal with a Los Angeles based producer. It wasn't a big deal by Hollywood standards, but a deal's a deal. And in the gee-I-hope-I'm-writing-these-pages-for-actual-pay world, where the vast majority of practitioners never see a dime from their efforts, I was able to bank a bit of dough. Over time I continued to write screenplays for pay. Heck, even a few were produced. Later, I had my first novel published, as well as a series of novelettes derived from that original novel's storyline.

The first request to read another writer's work came just a few months after that first screenwriting success. The request originated from a woman I'd known from a local amateur filmmaking community, so I was familiar with her and her burgeoning professionalism. I was happy to help.

Check that. I was more than eager to help because there was one thing I did not have when I started out and that was a mentor. Well, that's not entirely accurate. I didn't have a personal mentor that I could call on when I had made an errant turn into a writer's cul-de-sac.

I started into the writing world absent the USC/and/or/UCLA writing education, but not with a lack of creativity. The guidance I acquired early on originated from an immersion into the fictional worlds of writers like Elmore Leonard, Donald Westlake and Kurt Vonnegut. That's where I began finding my way through the vast domain of character, story and structure. Watching films from screenwriters and directors like David Mamet and Martin Scorsese helped me to find my way. So I guess I did have a few mentors – they just happened to be one-dimensional and constructed of paper and celluloid. It was a one-way street of informational sharing, but at least I didn't have to buy them lunches. The used bookstores, bargain matinees and Amazon VHS/DVD sales had their hooks into me, though. Big.

For the better, and admittedly at the very start, mostly for the worse, writing page after page – after page (!) - of crappy scripts and prose was my writing 'guru.' There's really no surer way of hitting your stride as writer than to, well – write.

Could I have used a real live mentor to help guide me back in those days? Yes, of course. But I truly don't believe now that I was savvy enough back then to even seek out any sort of guidance from professionals. It wasn't that I was cocky and didn't think I needed the help. I certainly needed the assistance. The simple truth was that, again, I just never considered asking anyone. And if it did ever cross my mind to dive in for the 'ask,' I probably shoved the thought quickly to the side with a 'there's no way in hell that writer so-and-so would ever respond to my request for guidance.' Simply put, I lacked the intestinal fortitude to even ask.

But my ego puffed with pride the very first time I was asked to help another writer. I barely knew what I was doing, but that person thought I had something going on and could help them. That was good enough for my ego…um, me.

I remember, though, another thought striking me at that time.

Something with a deeper emotional meaning was at play when that first writer approached me. They were stepping out of their comfort zone to ask someone they deemed to be more advanced in their chosen profession for help. That takes a lot of guts. A lot. Guts I never had when I started out. Anyone they approached could have easily told them no, or worse, ignored their request altogether. I think I admired that trait more than anything else -- so I said yes.

From time to time, but hardly every time, I've said yes over the past several years. The requests I turned down were mostly from people seeking to have me do their writing for them. They were folks who approached me with the age-old proposition, "I've got the greatest idea ever. You write it and we'll split the money." 9.9 times out of 8, the ideas were not that fantastic. Also, I never enter into agreements like that – for free.

Over the years I've developed an inner radar system that has allowed me to weed out the hangers-on, the 'something for nothing' practitioners, and find the true writing enthusiasts.

Like the time seven years ago when a 60-year old newly minted screenwriter I met in California asked for me to read and comment on his very first effort. The only reason I agreed was that the person had an affable and approachable personality. I was intrigued as to how he would attack the page with his writing, so I said yes.

And I was not disappointed. It was one of the rare occasions I had of finding a first timer who was able to place their personality directly on the page right out of the gate. Anyone who's been at the writing game for any length of time will tell you that you're making professional strides when you finally drop the stilted/unnatural/boring writing style of a newcomer. (Rule number one for writers: Never be boring.)

The 60-year old writer's story was fresh and intriguing, with real-life-lived criminal elements that I found fascinating. We spoke from time to time, had a lunch or four along the way, and a year later I was pleased to learn that he had placed as a semi-finalist in a well-respected screenwriting competition - and this with his very first screenplay ever. Shortly after that he found an agent willing to take him on as a client. Age-schmage.

I didn't write the man's work for him, I simply read, commented on what I observed in the work, listened to his concerns, and answered his questions. Any idea or bit of advice I give is offered with the proverbial grain of salt. Take it or leave it. It's the writer's story, not mine. I was there to be their sounding board. To help them work through some rough road.

Another acquaintance is a successful tech writer in Silicon Valley. Check that, tech writer at the moment - screenwriter/author in the making. His coming of age story about a phenomenal female athlete had some Hollywood eyes on it a while back, and then things dissolved, as they tend to do in the movie business. After many, many conversations on the story's direction, avenues to take while trying to get the project purchased by a producer, etc., my writing buddy hit upon another solution. He is now adapting the screenplay into a series of short stories to be published (serial-style) over a six-month stretch of time. Genius. His 'baby' won't die the slow death he had begun to envision for it when the Hollywood trail had grown cold. And who knows, now that it'll be out in the world, Hollywood may come calling again in the future. It could happen. I've seen stuff like that in the movies.

A Boston-area writer and I have been conversing on the phone for years discussing various elements of his work. We'd met online through his (now defunct) blog. This is a person with that intriguing mix of professionalism and a humble approach to his writing that I find fascinating. He's not a boastful person in the least. He just modestly shrugs and then proceeds to kick you in the literary teeth with his product. Two years ago he gave me a screenplay to read that I fell in love with. It was not perfect, but the story was incredible, believable, and emotionally compelling. He's honed his story over the past year or so and I'm happy to report that a major producer is interested in his tale now. I was just a sounding board for the writer on a few occasions, but I'm glad to be along, in a minor way, for his ride.

Another New England-based writer I met four years ago located a short story from a British writer and worked a deal to adapt the work into a feature length screenplay. The project was produced into a feature film and is being released this fall. Again, I didn't help this person write their work. I just loaned out my writer's brain every so often so ideas could be bounced to-and-fro, that's all.

I receive a lot of satisfaction in lending an ear and a writer's eye to other scribes. But the root of the satisfaction runs deeper than seeing their successes play out at IMDb or on Amazon. From experience, I know that a lot of time and effort goes into getting writing projects completed. For most of the time the writer is working for no pay. Zip. Actually – at the start of a career, it's all of the time that a writer is working for no money. All creative people start out this way. And although their friends and family may say they support them, they oftentimes don't. And that makes for a very lonely uphill climb.

So here's why I'm so passionate about helping other writers; whatever minor assistance I offer is not altruistic.

You probably saw that one coming.

I've discovered that the bits and pieces of advice I have acquired do not only help the other writer, they help me, too. Every time I speak with a writer seeking professional advice, the 'wise' words that I offer are served out of my big mouth, right back through my own ears, and seep ever so gently into my very own brain. It's that old 'rubber and glue' bit from the third grade all over again. Only this time I am the rubber. I am the glue.

As a writer, I am in constant need of continual swift kicks to my creative pants.

This is how passion is supposed to work. At least this is how my passion plays out. You help a certain someone and by helping them you help yourself. It's a win-win of the highest order.

To confess again, I didn't want to write this chapter of the book. I was invited to submit, and considered the proposition, but then let it fall by the wayside. Please don't misunderstand. It was an honor to be asked to contribute for the book. But then I got to thinking -- "who wants to read about my passion? Who am I to even write about passion?"

A few days ago, a writer I know who's originally from the Midwest called. He's an individual who went way out on a limb to chase his creative dreams and who now lives in California. He called to discuss a screenplay that he's been writing over the past year. I started getting a bit frustrated with the writer when he said he was stopping his process. I called him out and gave him a verbal kick in the pants, hoping it would spur him on. I wasn't mean-spirited, just plain and frank in my opinion.

As I yammered on, spewing my 'advice' to this fellow, cajoling him not to stop his process and to keep moving forward, it hit me.

Before that phone call from the California writer, I had been trying to avoid writing this chapter because well… again, who am I to write about passion?

Then I wondered how many speculative literary works would never had existed had it not been for one writer mentoring/cajoling another. Or how many students would have given up on their education had it not been for the guidance of an excellent teacher unwilling to give up on them.

Passion is a perpetual motion machine.

Passion was ingeniously designed to continuously kick people in their creative butts, and get them moving. It was built to never stop. When one person's passion wanes, another takes over and the constructive pants kicking continues.

When one individual mentors another they're really just mentoring themselves. And all it takes for that perpetual motion passion machine to spark to a start is for someone to say yes.

About the author:

Matt Hader is a novelist, screenwriter, and producer. In addition to the several screenplays he's written, optioned, and sold, Matt has also worked as a producer, and creative consultant on various film and television projects.

His novel *Bad Reputation* was published in 2011 and several *Bad Reputation* universe novelettes about various side characters will be published in 2013.

He currently makes his home in the Chicago area.

Matt Hader's novel *Bad Reputation* can be found at Amazon, Barnes & Noble, Kobo Books and other fine booksellers.

A Life of Passion(s)

By Hardie Karges

I'm not a motivational speaker or self-help guru, by trick or trade, profession or predilection, so to be invited to submit to the latest issue of this series, as if any insight or wisdom I might have acquired over the years might help someone else, is indeed an honor and a pleasure. If I can help just one person do one thing to make his life better, then it's all worthwhile. People need help. The world needs help.

If I can help, then I'm happy to do so. For the record, I'm just a guy, but something of a perpetual seeker, and sometimes even a finder (and I'll confess to a sneaky curiosity as to whether I can actually pull this off, I who sometimes seems helpless to make sense of his own life, I the guy soon turning sixty with growing pains still).

I do keep loosely apprised of developments in the self-help and motivational fields by listening to afternoon radio on some of my favorite public radio stations, so I am not totally oblivious to the trends and tendencies making the rounds. Some of these I agree with and some I don't. Sometimes I'm just a contrary s-o-b. Sometimes I play the devil's advocate. Most times I just don't know. No one does. At least I'm honest. I DO know what has worked best for me over the years, though.

My only professional qualification for this mission might be my degree in philosophy, but that's the academic sort, not the self-help sort, though it can be used that way. I did. I couldn't afford therapy, so I majored in philosophy (and my motto was something like "Plato not Prozac" long before the book of that name). Did you know that one of the greatest debates in the history of philosophy and religion is that of free will versus determinism? There is the hand you're dealt and the hand you play. The intersection of free will and determinism is you.

For some people the passion in life is simple—kids, grandkids, etc., back to the beginning of time. No finer work exists, either, but it didn't happen that way for all of us. Neither did the paradigm of the corporate career track, something everyone is so proud to have…and leave. But I never resigned from a corporate position, because I never had one. I never wanted one. I've hardly ever had a 'real job', though I've always worked very hard and never depended on anyone else to support me. For most of my life, I've lived by my wits and my whims, for most of which I had little formal training.

I know my mission here is supposed to be to fire you up to find and follow your passion, but I'd like to take a bit different tack, if you don't mind. That just doesn't match my experience. For me it's not so much 'A' passion to be found, but a lifetime of passions to be played out. For me it's not so much a revelation as recognition of what it is that ignites me, even though it may not have been a conscious decision.

In short, I didn't have to find my passions; they found me. Plural. Third person indicative. For starters: words, language, travel, nature, film, music, culture, anthropology, linguistics, physics, microbiology; the list continues on to infinity in no certain order. My problem is focusing on one at the time. How does one decide, when confronted by a multiplicity of passions? Listen to yourself. What do you talk about and think about when you're not strictly working at a 9-to-5 job or being entertained?

What feels good? What feels right? Which one path combines the greatest number of the passions and goals together under one roof? I started traveling at an early age, and never felt better than when I was doing so and even incorporated it into my career. It's only been recently that I've seen it as a vocation in and of itself (and it's great therapy, too). For until recently, I've always combined traveling with business, creating and dealing in world handicrafts and folk art. Now I realize that I was combining three (or more) passions into one—travel, (foreign) language, culture…and business.

My desire to write never went away. So now I write—and publish—travel books, currently offering a series of hostel guides to the world. I've never taken a course in business, yet done business all my life. I've never even taken a course in English composition (I passed the test in advance, so didn't have to), but now I'm a writer and publisher. I won't tell you that I'm working on my first billion, or even million, in sales or dollars, because it doesn't matter.

Success is always nice, but that's a sliding scale. By the way, no, my current project didn't go exactly as planned, so I made changes when I realized that declaring myself the next Paul Theroux, with the Great American Travel Book, would be difficult without some sort of, uh, 'platform,' to stand on. You gotta' be flexible. For me, art is the paradigm, not financial success. I want to do something unique and creative, not save one million souls or sell one million bowls (though that would be nice).

Many advisers would say to never compromise your passion, or your goals. I'd advise you to compromise them constantly, adjusting, making changes appropriate to changing circumstances. Not one of us lives in a vacuum, after all. We live in a specific place and time, and if you want to make a contribution, then it must be a 'fit.' That is the ultimate goal, isn't it, to make a contribution? What is the *Zeitgeist*, the 'spirit of the times'? How can you fit in? You adjust your goals. But you should never give up on them.

Many advisers would say never do anything halfway. I'd say do everything halfway, absolutely everything. Those halves can be cumulative, not divisive, a whole more than the sum of its parts, not a constant division, diminishing toward a vanishing point. Those halfway points can be stepping stones to something greater, or a turning point to something different and better, or an easier return if you've made a mistake. We all make mistakes. The greatest fool is the one who worries about making a fool of himself.

Some see a cup half empty, others see a cup half full; I see a cup in perfect balance. A carpenter's level tells you nothing without a bubble in the center (carpentry was my first profession, by the way). All water or no water is useless. Some people want bliss, which for me can lead to its opposite—sadness. Some people want great wealth, which can lead to its opposite—poverty... or at least that feeling. I want balance. I don't want to get lost in my passions, but rather learn by them. I personally don't want One Big Passion, but a lifetime of little passions, all in a row, all in a circle. Mostly I want to be at peace and in some sort of sync with the world.

Life can proceed by offense or defense, constructing it by adding one piece at the time or carving it out of one solid block, positive space or negative space. Personally my life has probably been more defensive in nature, protecting what I have, and constantly expanding, with incremental gains, and few risky offensive maneuvers. I never felt like I had much margin for error, i.e. money. It's only later in life that I've grown more comfortable throwing some long balls and doing some end runs.

I try to look for the highest common denominator in my life, not the lowest. What is the most important thing that you consistently aspire to, not the thing that you usually 'settle for?' Money is usually our lowest common denominator. But how much do you need to survive, thrive, and continue working for your highest goals? My policy is to strive for the highest goals possible while making at least the minimum amount of money I need to survive ... and thrive. How's that for creative capitalism?

Ask yourself direct questions. What can you contribute? What are your passions (plural)? Where do you live? What era do you live in? What activity can unite all the disparate units? How can you weave everything into one giant tapestry of (a) life? What has meaning? How can you enhance that meaning? Life may or may not have ultimate meaning, but we, as humans need it. This is primal, pre-linguistic.

Even animals see cause and effect and live their lives that way. Does a bird ask where it will sleep and what it will eat? You bet it does (though not in so many words). It asks for its offspring, too. This is primal nature, common to all animals, to take care of itself and its family. Religion and society attempt to enlarge that family. The popular advice to 'be here now' is fine once the means to survival are under control, and it's a perfect antidote for the stressed-out Wall Street gambler betting on the futures market.

As a philosophy major in college, one of my favorite focuses (foci?) — after Plato — was the study of Buddhism, a philosophy as well as religion and something of a welcome relief after the sometimes grinding tour through the British Empiricists and the Continental Rationalists — almost another version of the free will/determinism debate: Locke, Berkeley, and Hume versus Descartes, Spinoza, and Leibniz … or something like that. It's been a while.

Then I lived for ten years in Thailand, where I was surrounded by Buddhism and was exposed to much of the local variety of folk animism/Buddhism and was even married in a Buddhist ceremony. It's interesting to compare and contrast the academic book study and the practice of it in a loosely educated Third World country with one foot planted firmly in each of a rural superstitious past and an indeterminate high-tech future.

For while the average Asian may know little or nothing of even the most basic tenets of Buddhism — the Middle Way or the Four Noble Truths or the Eight-Fold Path — there is one thing they all do know: the *Law of Karma* (all monks know the full philosophy of course). Now the word 'karma' (it simply means 'actions') has been hip in the Western alternative press for at least a half century and that version of it is fairly accurate, but a point or two is worth repeating: by doing good deeds, good things will come to you, **but not as a direct result**. This is not simple give-and-take or cause-and-effect, mechanical and easy. It is a metaphysical principle. The same holds true for 'bad karma.'

I like it. Tweak it a little and you've got Jesus' Sermon on the Mount: "Love your neighbor as yourself," or Confucius, or Muhammad, or Lao-tzu, or just the basic Golden Rule: "Do unto others as you would have them do unto you." All of the religions hold special truths and they all hold this one truth. Put them all together and you've really got something, equal to or greater than all the scientific output of the last 1,500 years, I'd say.

Too bad we can't accept them all as equal and cumulative, rather than mutually exclusive. Kids should be Muslims, disciplined and single-minded; young adults should be Christian, ready for love and full of ideals; and senior citizens should be Buddhists, wise and reflective, non-possessive, ready to renounce a world that will soon end anyway. Unfortunately it doesn't work that way. But it should, IMHO (and I'm sure it's no accident that we of Christian culture are referring to "passion" as the highest goal, as opposed to duty or worldly renunciation).

Over the years, and in the course of personal trials and tribulations, I probably made a lot of promises to a lot of Gods, and maybe even invented a few new ones to hedge my bets ... many of which I've maybe forgotten. But one thing I do remember is that I always promised that I would devote more time and space to helping other people. And I intend to do that. This is hopefully a start. Every field of endeavor for me from now on will hopefully carry a socially responsible aspect.

Other passions that I plan to play out are in the field of language, for which I seem to have a love and a lust ... and hopefully some skill. I want to write more and better and with content that has meaning. To be able to do it in more foreign languages would be nice. I'm sure there will be many surprises along the remainder of this path. I might even go overboard, deciding to learn every language (or at least one per year). Ha!

Other possibilities depend on circumstances and opportunities. Very few of them depend on money. After all, once the kids are out of the way, the basic necessities of life (with the possible exception of health care and subject to changing expectations) are ridiculously easy to acquire for a Westerner from a developed country. What are your highest common denominators? What is the greatest and best thing that you might accomplish as long as the basic needs of your survival are already being fulfilled?

Then that is the thing that you should do. If you're still not sure, then make an old-fashioned list of things that inspire you and stimulate you. Rank them in order of importance from 1 to 10. Now rank them in order of the possibility for fulfillment, once again from 1 to 10. Add the totals. Which item has the highest combined score? Start there. How will you go about achieving that goal? Do you need to take a class? Do it. Classes are fun. You're never too old to learn.

If you're like me, then you may be a bit of a worrier and overly concerned about some of the details and minutiae of all this. That's probably okay. We are human, after all, as long as the concern stops short of stress. Stress is a killer; I know that (and I'm not even a medical doctor). Meditation is good and it works. Clean your mind of all the clutter, every last thought, once or twice a day. It's not easy, but eminently worthwhile. But I'm not the one to teach that. I'm learning myself. There are many teachers.

Be realistic (at the same time that you're being idealistic) with your goals and passions. Plan B's are good. Do you want to be President of the United States of America? You're going to need a Plan B. There's nothing wrong with that. I'm sure that every actual President had a plan B, too. Do you want to top Brad Pitt at the box office or Justin B on the Billboard charts? Keep that Plan B handy, and remember not to prescribe the outcome of your efforts. Those outcomes depend on other people's input. They've got the same free will/determinism stew going on in their lives that you do in yours.

Are you getting enough return on your investment in time, money and energy to continue with your current plan? Is it sustainable? If so, then you're good. If not, then maybe adjust your ultimate goal a notch—just one notch—and see if that makes a difference. If not, then maybe try another angle toward the same goal. That's the way of the warrior and the art of warfare, if I may channel Carlos Castaneda and Sun Tzu, respectively. Be willing to compromise positions as long as you're not compromising your ultimate goals.

Be flexible. But most of all: do not fear. Don't fear failure, of course. You already know that. But don't fear success, either. You'll know what to say if and when the President calls you up on stage to accept your award for saving the world. Or maybe you'll be the one handing out the award. Who knows? Keep that Plan A handy, too.

About the author:

American **Hardie Karges** took his first extended international trip at the age of twenty-one in 1975 and traveled to his first ten countries within two years, all for less than two thousand dollars. His first book, *Hypertravel: 100 Countries in 2 Years* was published in 2012. The full initial set of *Backpackers & Flashpackers: Guide to World Hostels* includes six volumes and will be completed by the end of 2013. Find out more at www.hypertravel.biz.

ADVENTURES OF THE NOT-SO-STAY-AT-HOME MOM

By Michelle Stien

Exactly five years ago I began my journey as a stay-at-home mom. It seems impossible that half of a decade has gone by since I chose to give up my career to raise my children. Yet, so much has happened and I've changed so much, it might as well have been 100 years ago.

I was selling advertising for a local newspaper when I got pregnant with my first daughter. My husband and I had been married for about three years and even though we knew we were ready to start trying, we still entered into it with apprehension. We had a wonderful life living as D.I.N.K.S. (Dual Income, No Kids). We hung out with our neighbors, went out to nice dinners and while we didn't do a whole lot of traveling, the option was still there.

We began trying to get pregnant, only to put it on hold after a few months due to some changes I had going on at work. Little did I know, I was already pregnant. That would be my first lesson in motherhood; no matter how much you plan, some things are just out of your control.

When Madelyn was six weeks old and I was still on maternity leave, my mom became very ill. She had lost several pounds and finally discovered she had a tumor the size of a cantaloupe in her abdomen. She had the tumor removed, but also had to have an ileostomy and colostomy. Luckily, the tumor was benign and there was hope that she could have both procedures reversed.

During that time, I was already an emotional wreck. Not only was I fearful that my mom might have cancer and watched her frail 75 pound body work to regain strength, I was struggling with postpartum depression. I had already dealt with and been treated for depression and anxiety for a good portion of my life, so I already had a plan in place with the help of my obstetrician.

Despite this and everything else going on around me, I tried to embrace and enjoy my time with my baby. We took walks every day even when I had to drive to my mom's house to take care of her. She hung with me during hospital visits, shopping trips for my mom's groceries and did her best to hold out for feedings between doctor's visits and long car rides.

Before I knew it, my 12 weeks of maternity leave was over and I was set to return to work. I was devastated and exhausted from the roller coaster ride of a maternity leave. I remember the night before I had to go back to work so vividly. I sat crying, holding my baby close and wondered how I could leave her at the daycare the next day. She just looked up at me and smiled. She had no idea.

In retrospect, I am thankful that God made it possible for me to be available to help my mom through her illness. I was the only one of my siblings who lived in the area at the time and could be there with her despite the fact I was tackling another major responsibility. I was able to manage it and it gave me a very interesting perspective on motherhood from the very beginning. I remember sitting in my mom's hospital room shortly after her surgery. I was nursing Madelyn and talking with my mom when it all became very clear to me how special a mother-daughter relationship truly is. I looked at my daughter, looked at my own mother and told her I never knew how much she loved me until I had a daughter of my own.

I returned to work and spent my entire first day crying. I hit a moment a quarter of the way through the day where I was able to function, but by three o'clock I knew I was pretty much worthless. I went to pick up my daughter at daycare and don't think I put her down for the rest of the day and night.

I had always thought I would be a working mom. I never saw myself as a stay-at-home-mom. I thought I could never trade my busy days at work where my mind was stimulated, I had goals and aspirations and a paycheck, for Sesame Street and play dates.

Then I had a child and my priorities shifted. I looked at my little creation each morning as I waved at her through the daycare window, and longed to stay home and watch her every move, watch Barney and play. I realized that what I thought was my "career" was really just a job. Of course, we weren't in a position for me to just up and quit my job to stay home. I still wasn't convinced I was cut out for staying home, but I definitely had a new goal and aspiration in mind. I wanted to find a way to spend more time with my child.

My husband and I knew we would have more than one child and soon it became clear that, while I made a pretty good living, two kids in daycare is expensive. I worked on commission and if I didn't make my goal, I barely made enough to make going to work worthwhile after paying for tuition. The newspaper industry wasn't doing so hot and I felt like much of what I did was an uphill battle. Never mind the fact that my heart wasn't into it because I was distracted my other responsibilities. Of course, part of those responsibilities involved taking my daughter to the pediatrician every six weeks because she kept getting sick from daycare.

My husband and I finally hit a point where he was up for a promotion and we were ready to start trying for number two. We decided it was time to pull my daughter out of daycare and I would stay home full-time. I thought about trying to go part-time, but my job didn't lend itself to that. Any part-time job I could find would pay much less and part-time day care isn't much cheaper than full-time. I took a deep breath and gave my notice.

Madelyn was fifteen months old and the perfect age for "Mommy and Me" type classes. I immediately signed her and me up for swim lessons. I cried during the first lesson because I saw her splashing in the water, smiling and laughing and knew that prior to that, she was "pretend swimming" on the dirty floor at the daycare. I knew I had made the right choice.

I had consulted a friend of mine, a fellow stay-at-home mom, before quitting my job and she told me the most important advice that I still refer back to every day. She told me I would never get this time back and that I would never regret it. And while I find myself having to remind myself of that sometimes, she was right.

I had barely gotten settled into my new life as a SAHM (now seasoned enough to use the acronym) when I got pregnant with my son. It made staying home taking care of a toddler a little more challenging, but once he arrived I was never bored or clock-watching for the day to be over. Colin Thomas came almost nine months to the day after my last day of work and the kids were 23 months to the day apart in age. It was hard to believe we actually made a conscious effort to get pregnant so soon after my daughter was born.

Needless to say, I didn't have as much time to focus on "what's next?" like I did when it was just my daughter and I. As much as I knew I had made the right choice, I still struggled with my new identity. I was a college graduate. I was the type of person who got recognized for their talents and abilities. I got promotions, accolades and saw myself becoming successful.

Now my accomplishments were much more simple; getting to eat a warm meal, taking a shower, leaving the house without baby food or breast milk on my clothes. Even more important, hugs and kisses, quiet moments where the kids snuggled on my lap, trips to the park and zoo. So many times I'd look at their little faces--their smiles, tears, runny noses or giggles--used to belong to someone else all day long. There were so many precious moments with my son Colin when he was an infant that I could not believe someone else got to share them with Madelyn.

There were certain things that I engaged in, in order to hold on to my own identity besides being a mom. The first was running. I began running regularly in my early twenties and eventually became what you would call an avid runner. I ran two marathons, a handful of half-marathons and more 5 and 10K's than I can count. Not only did I discover my love for the sport, but also over the years found out I was actually pretty good at it. I finished at the top of my age group at most local events I participated in. I loaded the kids in a double jogging stroller and ran as much as possible.

It not only kept me sane and started out as "me time," but it also became "us time."

I also volunteered on a 5K Committee through my old job and remained on it even after I stopped working. Many times I brought the kids with me to meetings and struggled to focus, but it helped me retain some of my communications, marketing and planning experience while supporting a worthy cause. Through the people I met on this committee, we created two more 5K charity runs supporting various local organizations. I had found my niche planning, promoting and organizing races.

I began to realize how good it felt to engage in these types of activities that focused on my talents, and it motivated me to continue to seek out things I could do to capitalize on my gifts. While I had become more comfortable with my role as stay-at-home mom, I felt like I needed more.

First up, I obtained my group fitness certification. After having the materials for three years and barely cracking a book, I finally committed to a test date, hit the books and got certified. Over the next two years I added various certifications and now I teach Spinning®, Pilates, Insanity!®, PiloxingTM and various other formats. This gave me a chance to combine my love of fitness and exercise with public speaking. It also gave me yet another chance to engage with other adults and I truly enjoy helping people reach their goals.

I was on the Speech team in high school and college and majored in Public Relations and minored in English. That led to my next step in using my talents. I signed up to be a lector at church. I used to do readings as a child and teenager since I went to Catholic school. So when my church conducted their annual "Time and Talent" campaign, I signed up and before I knew it I was up in front of the entire congregation several Sunday's out of the year. It also helped to renew my faith and get me back to going to church on a regular basis.

However, of all the things I sought out, I think the most important step I took was taking was writing. I had always wanted to write, but working always got in the way. Sure, I wrote sales reports and presentations at most of the jobs I had, but it wasn't writing for me. I used to think I should write while I was on the train when I commuted into the city. Yet, somehow I never had anything to write about.

Once I had my kids, I had plenty to write about. I would often call my mom and tell her my trials, tribulations, moments of hilarity and sheer joy over whatever happened with the kids did that day. She would always tell me I needed to "write this shit down." (Although she maintains she said "stuff.") And that's just what I did. I started a blog by the name "Write This Sh!t Down" and began telling all the stories about my kids including the funny, disgusting, frustrating, joyful, sentimental and amusing. I wrote about the things that no matter how many parenting books I read, the solutions were never easy. I wrote honestly and shot straight from the hip. No flowery, glossy portrayals of life with two toddlers. No sugar coating the amount of puke, poop and pee that I had to deal with on a daily basis between two kids, two dogs and a cat.

I felt like many parents out there were living this life every day despite their efforts to grin and bare it, afraid to admit we none of us have a clue as to what we are doing. I bared my soul, my flaws, my beliefs, my love for my children and family and it seemed that most of the people who read it could relate.

I posted my blog on Facebook and lived for the feedback. It gave me the sense of accomplishment that I needed. Soon, my former employer contacted me and offered me a column in one of their magazines. It started small in only one area and I didn't even get paid, but it was a chance to get published outside of my blog. Within a year, my column began appearing in three of the companies publications followed by a fourth a few months later. I would get calls, texts and Facebook posts from friends of mine who had read my article while they were in the doctors' office and happened to pick up one of the magazines. I also started to actually get paid for what I wrote.

Somehow, without really having a real plan, I found myself doing all the things I loved--being a mom, an athlete, a writer and a speaker. It took sifting through several aspects of my life amidst diaper changes and preschool drop offs in an effort to find time for myself. I traded spa days for Spinning® seminars. I took the risk of sharing what I wrote and fear that no one would read it or like it. I dug deep into who I really am at my innermost core and let it all hang out. What I found was that while I had certainly grown up and matured, especially since having children, all the things I was passionate about were at the root of who I was and who I had always been.

Now, don't get me wrong. I know that not everyone is fortunate enough to be able simply quit their job to stay home with their kids. I am very blessed that I was able to do so, but it wasn't without struggle and sacrifice. My journey hasn't been without bumps, bruises and failures along the way. I have set out on some projects, only to find myself backing away because they caused me to sacrifice too much in the name of my family. The bottom line is unlocking your talents takes discipline. It means taking risks. It requires getting up and out and doing things.

I also see other moms who have jobs and seem to be balancing success and motherhood, but I know full well the grass is always greener. I know that they struggle with balance and look at me and probably wish they had what I have. There are times my husband tells me about women he works with or one of his friends' wives who has a successful career and kids. I have to ask him if he wishes I were like them. He, without skipping a beat, says "no." He values my role in this home and knows that the time I did work helped to buy our first home, pay for our wedding, pay off our student loans and establish a pretty solid 401(k).

So, while my blog hasn't become a household name nor do I make any money off of it, I've expanded my writing and now here I am writing an excerpt for this book. While I haven't published any of the books that I have set out to write, it doesn't mean I won't someday.

I remember when I was working I would sometimes hide in the local Starbucks to do paperwork. One day I saw a group of women with their young children. The women were socializing while the children kept to themselves (at least from what I recall). I looked at them and missed my daughter terribly. I wished so badly I was them. Then, I became them. And my trips to Starbucks weren't so glorious. They usually were a necessity since I was running on four hours of sleep due to one of the kids cutting a tooth. They involved yelling at my son not to knock over a display of coffee cups, French Presses and flavored syrup in glass bottles. If I was lucky enough to meet up with a friend, we were lucky to finish a single conversation.

While there are plenty of days I really wish I could sit at a desk and have a moment of solitude, I do not regret quitting my job for a minute. I'm so grateful that we are in a position for me to stay home. Being a mother is the hardest, most challenging job I have ever had. Sometimes I feel guilty that I need more, but I know if I'm not happy, there is no way my family will be.

While my aspirations have us in constant motion, my fulfillment is to their benefit. It involves a lot of sacrifices, but in the end I get to continue to be with my kids while pursuing things that I am truly passionate about. I used to think that staying home limited me from accomplishing great things, now I feel like it is the reason I am able to accomplish great things.

About the author:

Michelle Stien is a stay-at-home mom with two children, Madelyn, 6 and Colin, 4. She and her husband Tom live in Algonquin, IL. In addition to raising her children and blogging, Michelle is a columnist for Shaw Suburban Media magazines; *Lake County Magazine*, *McHenry County Magazine*, *Kane County Magazine* and *Suburban Life Magazine*. She is also a group fitness instructor at Lifetime Fitness, Dundee Township Park District and Melt Pilates and Hot Yoga. You can read more on Michelle's blog at www.writethishitdown.blogspot.com.

A Dream Delayed is Not a Dream Denied

By Lorraine M. Castle

BRIGHT BEGINNINGS BECOME DILUTED

I have been writing for as long as I can remember. My love of reading came before my love of writing. My mother loved reading. Her first real job was as a librarian. It was through her love for reading that I was introduced to Golden Books and Mother Goose Nursery Rhymes. I also had Golden Records that were really yellow and sometimes orange and my own little record player. I would play the records for hours on end as I memorized and recited the nursery rhymes.

As children will often imitate based on their surroundings, I began writing my own stories and poems. The stories came natural and had a beginning, middle and an end replicating what I observed in the books I read. The poems, though fun to write, were more challenging. They did little more than rhyme and most often didn't make sense to an adult, but they were fun for me as I did what I began to love – write stories and poetry.

When I won a writing contest at the age of eight or nine, one would have thought that I would certainly follow my love for writing throughout my lifetime and career. That was far from the truth.

Because we moved five times from my age of six through twelve, I found it difficult to develop close friendships. I was shy and fading from the limelight became a coping mechanism designed through the necessity of always being the new kid on the block. I was often the target of bullies and the brunt of jokes.

The writing contest that I won was a homework assignment. Putting my feelings on paper had become a substitute for the lack of close friends. I didn't have an invisible friend. I had my pen and paper. I don't recall the topic of the paper, but I do recall that I described an experience that impressed my eight or nine-year-old self. The assignment became the writing contest and I won! I won a book – I think the name of it was The Little Pony. Ironically, the book was lost during a move as an adult.

The second part of the "prize" was for me to read my paper in front of the entire auditorium! The last thing I wanted to do was read my "winning" paper in front of peers – most of whom I did not know very well and many of who were the same bullies that taunted me at the end of each school day.

Midway through reading my paper, came the intimate sections that were the reason for my win. It was embarrassing and children being children, I began to hear snickers throughout the auditorium. I was horrified. This experience was so traumatic to me that it placed a stigma on sharing my writing with anyone.

A Dream Delayed

While I continued to write, most of what I wrote was for my eyes only. Every now and then, I would share my poetry with a family member. I received compliments from my family telling me that I would soon become a best selling author. It was encouraging to hear this, but they were family. They had to say they enjoyed my writing – whether they did or not.

I earned an "A" for every article I wrote for school assignments. As I completed high school and eventually went on to college, I continued to receive compliments about my writing skills. I will say those compliments did encourage me, but not to the point where I was ready to share my writing with the world.

I subconsciously constructed a barrier where writing was concerned. School counselors suggested colleges that I could attend, but I wanted no part of it – at the time. I believed entering the business world was a safe retreat for me. In my mind, it was the opposite of writing.

I found myself majoring in Accounting and Finance. I flourished in this field and spent the next 40 years working my way up from a mail clerk to middle management. I took evening classes at local colleges. I did well, but there was no passion. One does not have to be passionate about something in order to excel in that area. My desire to excel propelled me along, but there was no passion in my daily activities.

ACKNOWLEDGING THE VOID

Lacking passion, I filled my void with work, school and eventually, marriage. Something was missing, but I couldn't define the void that I felt. After sixteen years, my marriage ended. I was single again. I was childless. I was alone. I moved to a different state – to an area where I only knew one person. The person that I knew had a hidden agenda, so I soon found myself in an area that was foreign to me – and I was alone. I wasn't too uncomfortable with this situation because during my lifetime, I had become a bit of a loner.

During this transitional period in my life, I continued to fill my time (void) with work. Divorce and moving to another state depleted my finances; so continuing my education was no longer an option. I worked fourteen hour days, went home to my four walls and I began to write in journals. I poured my heart out onto blank paper that was at times stained with my tears.

This is not a sad story. This is a story of the release and growth of passion. This is to educate those who do not know – who have not realized – that a void within your spirit must be filled. It can be filled with things of the world – such as alcohol or drugs. It can be filled with a precarious lifestyle. I will be the first to tell you that while I tried to fill this void with work and school, there were also times when I strayed to the dark side. None of these vices is permanent or everlasting.

Attempting to fill a void caused by not living your passion is futile. The void becomes a bottomless pit and nothing will complete you until you've faced your demons – whatever they are.

Passion fills my void. Passion fuels my dream. Though ignored by me, my passion to write remained within me and it was fighting to be revealed. Unrealized passion and an unfulfilled dream can create a huge void within your soul.

A New Beginning

One day I was invited to a local church. I joined the church on my first visit and became active in the Music Ministry by joining the Choir. The church was putting on a Christmas play and the Choir was singing throughout the play. During the rehearsals, I was mesmerized. I attended as many of the rehearsals as I could. I couldn't explain what drew me to the rehearsals. In hindsight, I realize it was my passion for writing that drew me.

For months after the play, I felt a pull to join the Drama Ministry. I couldn't believe what my inner self was suggesting! There was no way that I was going to put myself in the position of appearing before a church full of people and performing. Interestingly enough, singing on the Choir did not have the same negative effect on me as performing on stage with the Drama Ministry. I didn't understand the pull to join the Drama Ministry. The feelings of the eight or nine year old Lorraine rushed back into my psyche. I could feel the battle going on within me.

One Tuesday evening I went home and changed out of my work clothes and since I wasn't going anywhere, I put on my pajamas. As I settled in for the evening, the "nagging" began. I could hear my inner voice urging me to go to the Drama Ministry meeting. I spoke to that inner voice saying, "Not now." As clearly as if the voice was in the room with me, I heard, "If not now, when?" That question was enough to get me to change my clothes and go to the Drama Ministry meeting.

Once I arrived at the meeting, I was shocked to realize that the Drama Ministry consists of two segments – actors and writers! Who would've known? I guess I should have realized there would have to be writers, but it's amazing what fear will do and how fear can distort what is real.

Renewed Passion

For the first time, I was in the presence of other writers. I was in so much denial and kept my writing abilities so well hidden, that I now realize I was also keeping myself from an entire community of writers. Joining the writing team was the beginning of my release and the beginning of the fulfillment of my passion to write. As a member of the team, I wrote for hours writing plays, skits, poems and devotions.

I truly felt like, for the first time, the void within me was beginning to be filled. Within a year, I became President of the Writing Team. A few years later, I was asked to teach Christian Writing 101 classes. I was in my element! I was in my element as I put together a writing curriculum and lesson plans for a full semester. I was also panicked because I felt unprepared until I realized that I had everything I needed to prepare and teach the lesson plans.

I was still working my 9-to-5 and working 12-14 hour days. My 9-to-5 became my means to make my ends meet. It was a living, but it was not my passion. It's important to know the difference. My job paid my bills. My passion filled my spirit and soul. Wouldn't it be nice if my passion could pay my bills? I asked myself that fleeting question every now and then.

Another Detour or a Blessing in Disguise

I was a member of the ministry for about 10 years. Eventually, my job took over more and more of my life and I left Drama Ministry. How many of us forfeit what is fueling our passion in exchange for something that will pay our bills? Don't get me wrong. We all have to eat, keep a roof over our heads, provide for our families and loved ones. When I think about how I left what I loved, so that I could work more unappreciated hours at my 9-to-5, it gives me pause and makes me wonder about my priorities. Was there a way I could have done both?

Life has a way of throwing curveballs. My mother and brother moved closer to me. They were previously about an hour from me. Now they were about 10 minutes away. This was good. I missed having family so close. A few years afterwards, Mom became ill. I believe she saw this coming and this was her reason for moving closer. At the end of 2007, we moved in together so that my brother and I could take care of Mom. A year later, I was laid off from my demanding job. I wasn't able to find another job because I was over qualified. Was this a blessing in disguise?

ANOTHER NEW BEGINNING

In 2009, I went back to school to finish what I had started some 20 years before. I majored in Communications. The major part of my courses involved writing. Additionally I was on a team with different team members each semester. It was during these team sessions that I realized that I was very good at editing and proofreading.

I needed to do something to earn a living. I realized that even though I continued to apply and interview for jobs in Corporate America, I really did not want to go back to that rat race. I began to think about my qualifications and considered working for smaller companies perhaps with less demanding requirements. I began to realize that many companies would still consider me overqualified.

Like many others, I've thought about working from home, but until 2010, I had not considered pursuing that profession. In August 2010, I researched the possibility of working from home as a virtual assistant. A virtual assistant performs duties similar to an executive assistant. While I had never been an executive assistant, I've worked with executive assistants who supported various teams. When layoffs and cutbacks began, the first position eliminated was often the executive assistant. Those duties often reverted to the manager. It was during my training to become a virtual assistant that I discovered the niche that I now serve as a Virtual Author's Assistant.

A Brand New Me

Today I am fulfilling my passion and living my dream. I'm writing! I can't believe that I'm writing. I have a blog, I write short stories and I write poetry. I'm working on a memoir. I am making much less money today than I did when I worked in Corporate America, but I am happier today. I feel fulfilled and I feel appreciated. There is no void in my soul. Doing what I love has filled that void.

Along with writing, my job as a Virtual Author's Assistant allows me to work with beginning authors and established authors as I help them to reach their goals. The tagline for my company is, "Your Success is my Goal." I understand the struggles of a writer. Identifying with the author gives me insight so that I can help them to resolve whatever roadblocks they may be facing.

Fulfilling Your Passion

I don't know if I've adequately explained the importance of fulfilling your passion. You will never know complete satisfaction until you've identified your passion and then strive to reach your passion. In some instances, you may not realize that you're smothering your passion. That's what happened with me. My passion was identified very early. I knew I enjoyed writing. However, coupled with that joy was the fear of speaking in front of an audience. I allowed that fear to drive me away from what I loved.

There is a misconception that if it's difficult, then it must not be your gift or your passion. I don't agree with that statement. While some qualities come to us naturally, in most instances, we must train and be educated, even in the area of our passion. In fact, the passion should drive you to learn more about your passion.

Passion Defined

What is your passion? Remember, a job is not necessarily a passion. Just because you're good at something, doesn't mean that you're fulfilling your passion. Passions are often identified when we are children. What gave you joy as a child? What activities came to you naturally? That activity may be where your passion lies. What I now realize is that fulfilling my passion gives meaning to my life.

When in Corporate America, I knew that the company would carry on with or without me. As a writer, I know that while someone else can write a story, only I can write my story – passionately and with passion!

A Dream Delayed but not Denied

I'm living my dream. I'm fulfilling my passion. My dream was delayed (I was my own worst enemy), but my dream was not denied. Following my passion allowed me to reach for the stars and live my dream!

About the author:

Lorraine M. Castle's passion is writing. Lorraine is a Virtual Author's Assistance and she shares her passion of writing as she assists authors with editing, proofreading, manuscript formatting, and eBook formatting and marketing their books. Lorraine has a blog www.castlevirtualsolutions.com/blog. Lorraine's company is Castle Virtual Solutions LLC where "Your Success Is My Goal!"

LEARNING TO UNLEARN

By Al Wilson

As children, we are raised to believe that justice will triumph in the end and that cheaters will get punished. I was drafted into the British army and learned that these are not truths. The army promotes junior officers who delight in exercising their power over new recruits. Even when you go up a level of the inspections on the parade ground, the Sergeant Major demonstrates the power of senior officers to impose a punishment to all on parade because of his perceived poor turnout of a few recruits. Then of course, when on a cross country march, the column avoids a deep mud puddle only to be marched back into it and have to "mark time" stamping up and down in it. The next morning you are expected to appear on parade with everything clean and shinny.

Through this, I was thinking about things "not being fair." I then realized, "who said it should be?" Of course the primary object of all this training is to teach you that, no matter how stupid or dangerous the command you are given, you will follow orders and charge the machine gun on the hill in front of you.

I hated the army but it did teach me a lot. I learned to accept stupidity and smile at the anger of others. Changing parade punishment was a good example. Your group of recruits was ordered to line up outside the barrack at an appointed time dressed in best uniform. The group would have to run around the parade ground and line up again. We were then told to change into physical training dress and that the last one back in line would get a dirty job. One more run around the square and then back for another change of clothing. This went on until the officer decided to have everyone dress back into their best uniform. They then found out that while running around the square he had gathered everyone's clothes into one huge pile at the end of the barrack room. To see grown men fighting and shouting because they could not find one of their boots and were going to get a dirty job taught me the futility of getting upset. If you ended up being the last one back outside, then that was just your bad luck.

I learned about innocence. Being asked by a fellow recruit what the flush on the toilet was for. He probably was a farm boy who had an outdoor toilet dug by his father. I was upset to see that on a trip to the store he was asked to get a tin of black boot polish for another recruit. On his return he was told, "I wanted dark black, not light black" and the guy went back to try to get it changed. I learned not to mock the less fortunate or less educated.

During my deployment to Jordan, in the Middle East, I learned there are good officers. We had a soldier who had re-enlisted because the recruiter had told him he would be better off in the army. He wrote a letter to the commanding officer saying that this was not true as he was being paid far less that he would earn as a civilian. The sergeant major saw him kicking wildly on the side the tent and asked what the problem was. "I am frustrated sir".

"Ok, kick away son," was his reply as he walked away.

I learned that water could make a decision! I had been told that the town of Aqaba experienced rain roughly every 7 years. On Christmas Eve I walked through the garrison to the barbershop to get a haircut. I could see distant lightning down the Red Sea Gulf but though nothing of it. Walking back to our camp it was getting much closer and as I neared the gate I heard what I can only describe as a frightening noise. I ran to the recreation hut and as I got there the heavens opened up. I sprinted to my tent and looking out through the screen door it was a green haze with nonstop lightening. I thought it was impossible to rain this hard and then it doubled in intensity! Six inches of water rushed across the tent floor and we had everything up on the beds including ourselves.

On weekends I had been exploring and climbing the mountains along the valley. I had seen canyons where the walls were 25 feet high and the floor 100 foot wide covered in sand with signs that water had previously been there. I figured that it had taken hundreds of years to form these canyons. Wrong! Seven inches of rain in one hour can do that! Needless to say our Christmas was shot! My 50 ton cold store had the mechanical room, with its diesel driven refrigeration equipment, flooded with water leaving everything buried under three feet of sand. My 10 ton cold store had floated away, the dry goods warehouse had filled with water and the walls collapsed outward, the airstrip was washed away and the wells were filled with debris and sand.

This started with our Royal Engineers detachment doing 2 days of nonstop frantic work to get basic services operating. The power generation equipment began operating again and the operation of some of the wells was restored. The one diesel engine that was not running at the time of the flood was dug out, opened up and washed out repeatedly with kerosene. We got going again so the garrison still had food. Sand from the beach was trucked to the airstrip where 32 wheel trailers with 70 ton Centurion Tanks mounted on them were driven up and down the strip while sand and salt water was spread in front of them. It took 10 days before a DC-3 airplane was able to land there. I learned about the power of water!

Both there and later when working in Africa I learned that, "In the valley of the blind, the man with one eye is king!" The king of Jordan had contacted the British government who had contacted the army headquarters in Cyprus who called my commanding officer who told me I was to be flown in King Hussein's private plane up to the Jordanian Air Force Base at Zerka to fix their refrigeration. In Africa I had installed air conditioning in three cinemas, a hospital emergency room, the Kenya currency vaults at a bank beside Mt Kilimanjaro and an insurance building.

Then Kenya was promised independence from British rule and the African politicians foolishly made many wild statements. The most foolish was that any monies loaned to the Kenya Government would be dishonored. Business died, there was no mortgage monies, stores sold what they had on their shelves and immigrants got their money out of the country leaving only enough for airline or tickets or berths on a boat to leave the country.

I had a promise of a contract to install air conditioning for another cinema but the owner did not want to spend the money and then got kicked out of the country. I had to return to England and had trouble finding someone else to take over responsibility for my installations. I ended up passing the job to an ex-General Motors carburetor expert!

I was fortunate to have had the opportunity to work in many different countries. Jordan. Russia, Lithuania, Malta, Germany, Kenya and Tanganyika. I have learned that people are the same the world over. They are the good, the bad, and the ugly! I have seen that basically there are only two types of people, Givers and Takers. I have found that you need to have a support group of givers.

My eye doctor/surgeon who has taken care of our family is also trying to preserve what little sight is left for a 92 year old lady neighbor that we try to take care of. On our last visit the doctor commented he had just returned from a trip. I asked where to and he said he had been in Cambodia!

"What did you go there for?" I asked. He said he had done two weeks of free cataract surgery where there was no other treatment location. He said that the patients were led in with a white stick. I said, "So you remove the totally frosted lens and replace it with a clear one? They must think you are god."

He said, "Yes, but can you imagine the wonderful feeling that gives me? It sets me up for another year here in my practice." He then said that this was his fifth visit there but would not be going again as his Cambodian assistant was now able to perform the surgery. My general practitioner doctor was a member of the "Doctors Without Borders" for many years; going to help in disaster areas. My dentist also has helped those who could not afford treatment. They are all GIVERS.

I now volunteer as a Site Steward at Dixie Briggs Fromm State Nature Preserve where for many years I provided a location where youngsters can perform their court assigned community service hours. I tell them that if they were washing police cars or cleaning the floors at the YMCA; they would be dirty again tomorrow. Instead they will be working to improve a nature preserve that will be there for them to show their children, and that they had a hand in making this place special. They should be proud of what they are doing.

At the end of the workday I call a halt and gather up the tools. Before we head back to the parking lot but I tell them, "Wait a minute."

They ask, "What for?"

"Look back. Did we get much done?"

"Wow we did a lot!" they say.

"Yes and how much would I have accomplished on my own? I thank you for your work, I appreciate the help."

They learn that the preserve is a very special place and some continue as volunteers. Upon completion I tell them that there will come a time when they are looking for a partner to share their life with. Try to remember what this old man told you. That if that person wants you to "Do this for them, take them to this event, buy this for them," etc. then that is a "Taker" and they would be much better off with a Giver!

"Paying it forward" is a tradition that I have learned, it is strangely reciprocal. When I have been able to help someone in difficulty and they have wanted to pay or reward me. I have always said that they should help someone else and pay it forward to restore the balance. It is strange but whenever I have been in trouble there has always been someone who came to my rescue.

Probably the best example was when I was driving my family from England to Russia, back when Khrushchev was their leader. In Poland, in my French Citroen, my gearbox exploded all across the street. I flagged down a passing car and with my Russian and his English he understood to take me in his car back to my hotel.

The manager there had an English customer who was could speak Polish and he got him to come and meet me. He set me up with some moonlighting mechanics that proposed to weld the aluminum casing back together. The communist government garage would have ordered parts from France, which would take weeks. Instead he loaned me his car to drive to West Germany, find a scrap yard where I could buy a second hand gearbox. I think that was a "pay it forward" event.

I helped a family who at night were off on vacation with their grandparents traveling in the camper towed behind the car. Bad weight distribution got the trailer wagging until it turned over on its side at the edge of the road. The police arranged to have the vehicle towed away and fortunately nobody was hurt. They were in need of help so I took them home and put them up for the night so that in the morning after breakfast they could call other family members to come and get them.

Life is definitely as good as you yourself make it. Be helpful to others and tolerant of their failings. Treat others as you would have them treat you and **BE A GIVER**.

Remember every day above ground is a good day!

About the author:

When **Al Wilson** was six years old WWII started. 80 years of living in troubled times have provided a great variety of experiences. He came to America in 1970 to evaluate a job offer prior to accepting it. Since then I have been trying to get Americans to speak English; he is not winning! Every year on Independence Day he throws the ceremonial tea bag into his creek and tries to make peace with the locals. He has met many wonderful people that he proudly calls friends. For over 30 years, Al and his wife Barb volunteered restoring the Prairie State's preserves.

You are welcome to email questions to LithFen@aol.com.

Mission to Passion

By Gwendolyn Koehler

A five minute phone call changed my identity. Who I had been for the last thirty years was no more. Although I did not realize then, the brutal force of that change launched me into the stormy process of reigniting my passion.

On the day of that phone call, I was halfway into a twelve month leadership academy. The academy kicked off six months earlier with a weeklong training. My colleagues and I were expected to take what we learned and implement it for a year, culminating with a follow-up retreat. In the interim, we would work with a mentor, complete assignments and record our reflections.

One of our tasks that first week was to develop a personal mission statement. Like other academy participants, I was familiar with work related mission statements. In fact, I had helped write organizational mission statements at various points in my career. During these experiences, I greeted the activity with moderate hope and enthusiasm. Sometimes I lamented the tedious process and privately questioned how it related to the more urgent parts of my job. Too often, I resented the time it took me away from those urgencies.

At other points in my career, I inherited a mission statement which was typically posted on a wall or website. When I accepted a new job, I usually gave a casual glance to this statement (rarely did anyone who hired me point it out) and dove into the day to day activities required of me. Seldom did I think about how the mission statement helped me deal with the multitude of tasks vying for my attention.

The academy facilitators led us through a process of writing a personal mission statement, unrelated to our specific job or organization. Mildly skeptical, I went along with the activity. The first step was to reflect upon, discuss and define our personal identities. We were a mixed group from several states. Different ages, marital status, and genders impacted the discussion and enriched it. Our conversation led us to the varied roles we played. Despite our differences, commonalities included who we were as daughters, sons, mothers, fathers, spouses, uncles, etc.

The most obvious roles were family roles such as a parent raising a child or a child turned caretaker of an aging parent. Others were outside of family and included roles in communities or churches. We recognized that sometimes we chose these roles; other times these roles were thrust upon us. Roles loomed large in our lives, and we structured our days around the responsibilities associated with them. One thing was clear. All of us tended to define our identity through these roles.

The facilitators suggested we rearrange that view. Roles tell us what we do, they explained. But should we permit our roles to define who we are? They asked us to look beyond the function of our roles in order to understand who we were and why we do what we do. We looked deep within ourselves to identify the values and principles by which we lived. These deeply held beliefs guide us in all we do and tell us why we do it. Based on these, not our circumstantially defined roles, we examined our real purpose in life — our mission.

To craft a personal mission statement, we spent more time reflecting and less time discussing. Unlike the participatory process of writing a work related mission statement, this process became a profoundly private activity. By the end, we used what we had learned about ourselves to articulate a deeply personal mission statement.

It was a gratifying and insightful week. Still, each of us felt the urgency to get back to our lives. On Friday, I hurriedly packed my notes, along with a week's worth of dirty clothes, to add to the papers and laundry that had piled up in my absence. I tucked my personal mission statement into my briefcase and forgot about it as I returned home to resume the many roles I played. I immediately focused on the responsibilities demanding my attention, and my personal mission statement became as invisible as the mission statement on the wall where I worked.

Six months later I was pondering when to start dinner after a long workday when the phone rang. The policewoman told me my beloved, fifty-two year old husband of thirty years was dead.

Life preserving numbness and treasured support of loved ones got me through the initial days and weeks following that phone call. Through pounding waves of pain, grief and endless death related details, I eventually drew in erratic breaths of insight. Somewhere in the fight to the surface of a new reality, I realized that how I defined myself for thirty years had changed. I was no longer a wife - the top of the list of my roles/identity. My husband had been at my side since I was seventeen, so I had never lived as an adult without him. Now I was a widow. His death made me a single parent.

With no father in the picture, it was up to me to reassure four children and teach them how to handle a loss I could not grasp. I became the sole breadwinner with three children in college. With no warning, I picked up the phone that night thinking I was one person and hung up as someone else.

In contrast to my personal life, my role at work had not changed, but it was enveloped in a fog. I would have gladly relinquished this role to deal with the dramatic changes in my personal life, but my new role as head of household gave me no choice. I had to go to work and perform my duties. One task was to catch up on a reflection paper for the leadership academy. My employer had paid for me to participate in the academy, and I had a responsibility to complete it.

Fuzzily, I reviewed the assignment. Less than a page. I could focus on that. Because the retreat seemed a lifetime ago, I dug out notes to refresh my damaged memory. Buried in forgotten papers I found my personal mission statement. As I read it, I was dumbfounded. Nothing about this personal mission statement had changed. Everything in my life had changed, but the vision behind these words had not. In the churning chaos I was living, that statement still made sense. In fact, it was the only anchor I found to hang on to.

That's what a good mission statement does. It anchors us in the midst of a storm. According to Steven Covey, our personal mission statement focuses on our "changeless core" and becomes our personal constitution that guides us in all we do. He says it becomes the source of our security, guidance, wisdom, power and becomes a basis for decision making. How welcome it was to discover something stable in my life. It became my beacon, guiding me as I struggled to survive. No longer was it lost in the back of my consciousness. It was front and center as I navigated through strong currents pulling me in new directions.

Throughout this journey, an ever changing emotional state possessed me. Passion was not one of them. My personal mission statement helped me put one foot in front of another. It helped me stumble forward, but I did so awkwardly, wearily and without passion.

Passion implies fervent enthusiasm. We are actively engaged with what we are passionate about. We are strongly connected to it. We gravitate to what we are passionate about because deeply felt zeal for specific activities makes us want to participate in them. People have passion for playing music, designing their home, supporting their favorite sports team or riding their Harley motorcycles. We envy couples that share and sustain a passion in their relationship.

We think of passion in terms of intense emotion, not going through the motions as I was doing. It is true that passion is typically sparked by a specific interest or personal preference. However, it is rooted in something deeper than an emotional state; it is rooted in a state of commitment. If grounded in such fertile soil, passion can grow. A sense of personal mission is that soil. Still, it needs more. We cultivate passion with the qualities required of us to successfully pursue our sparks of interests.

Discipline is the first manifestation of commitment. Discipline does not allow us the luxury of feeling one way or another. In fact, discipline disregards our feelings of being tired, cranky, or unmotivated. It instead drives us to what we have committed to do. It forces us to take action. Properly taken, action connects us to something and the resulting bond is the underpinning of passion.

Few students of music get excited about the unrecognizable sounds they hear when they first pick up an instrument. It is only with disciplined practice that they eventually produce the music that stirs their passion. On a daily basis passionate couples feel a variety of feelings about their spouse, including negative ones. But the discipline behind their commitment to one another keeps them engaged with each other. It is no coincidence that we say that couples that commit their lives to one another are "engaged." We see the manifestation of this daily commitment in the passion they exhibit.

Sacrifice is discipline's companion. We are more excited about something when we have sacrificed for it. It becomes more meaningful. Antoine de Saint-Exupery, the author of *The Little Prince*, says:

"Only he can understand what a farm is, what a country is, who shall have sacrificed part of himself to his farm or country, fought to save it, struggled to make it beautiful. Only then will the love of farm or country fill his heart."

When we sacrifice, we become invested in what we do. Within a balanced approach, we put aside wants that are of lesser importance to us - an extra hour of sleep, a TV program instead of a run - to achieve something of greater importance to us. The sacrifice involved elevates the value of what we have achieved.

Despite our commitment, despite our discipline and sacrifice, we will come across disappointment and obstacles as we nurture our passion. Sports enthusiasts know the disappointment of a lost victory. Motorcycle buffs traveling cross country encounter formidable weather. Yet, real enthusiasts have the fortitude to persevere despite challenging setbacks.

Diana Nyad, passionate about marathon swimming, tried five times over a thirty-five year period to swim the distance from Cuba to Florida. Her first attempt in 1978 was unsuccessful because of strong winds and resulting eight foot swells that slammed her into the sides of her shark cage. She abandoned the cage in subsequent attempts, but wicked weather, jellyfish stings, asthma and nausea prevented her time and again from succeeding. Finally, in September 2013, at age sixty-four, she accomplished her goal and became the first person confirmed to swim that distance without a shark cage.

By her fifth attempt, she was familiar with the obstacles and used what she had learned in previous attempts to overcome them. A submerged guide equipped with LED lights provided direction to keep her on course; a special mask and body suit helped protect her from jelly fish and man of war stings; her intentional added weight helped her deal with physical changes during the swim including loss of body mass, dehydration and hypothermia. Over thirty-five years, each setback and resulting redoubling of effort made the accomplishment more spectacular. Throughout any passionate endeavor, emotions waver. But the strength of character that is manifested through fortitude does not.

Passion has seasons and it requires patience. As time passed and the haze that enveloped my world began to clear, I questioned what motivated this new person I had become. I realized that as a wife, my passion centered in three areas: family, work and leisure time. Together my husband and I had passion for raising our children to be healthy and happy. Both of us were educators and together we shared a passion for the value of quality education.

In our limited free time, we shared a passion for theater. We went to the theater, we studied theater, we performed in theater and we had our own theatrical production company. So many elements of theater resembled what we valued. Like a family, cast and crew work together as a team to create something spectacular, bringing life to words. A dramatic presentation can educate, opening one's minds to new perspectives. We loved seeing the impact theater has.

As a widow, my passion for family did not change. In fact, it strengthened. But I learned what any single parent knows: without a partner, the day to day work requires greater endurance. My passionate conviction that education changes lives never faltered. In fact, education helped me to survive. My education allowed me to have a career that supported us. It opened new doors to new opportunities as well as new ways of thinking. I needed to educate myself about grief, widowhood, legal and medical issues. For me, the process of reigniting my passion for family and education happened naturally, although slowly, within a new context.

Other parts of my life remained lifeless. I wondered if I would ever again be interested in theater. Only a few days prior to his death, my husband and I had performed together. After his death I received requests for performances with someone else filling the role he played. How could I ever revive my passion for these performances when memories of what I lost pained my bruised and battered feelings?

I accepted that my wounds were too raw for the type of theater we did together. It was not the right season. Eventually, I found the courage to participate in a different type of theatrical production. Unsure of what emotions I would uncover in the process, I made the commitment. In the weeks leading up to the performance, I was consumed by a process that required the discipline of memorizing seventy pages of lines and sacrificed all free time as we rehearsed late into the night. "The show must go on" mentality propelled us through setbacks such as illnesses and last minute changes. If I did not feel passion when I committed to doing the performance, I certainly felt it as cast and crew embraced and congratulated each other behind the curtain following the audience's appreciative applause.

Rediscovering my personal mission statement allowed me to rediscover my passion. My family structure changed, my job changed, where I lived changed and how I spent my time changed. Behind the scenes of each of these was the stabilizing force of my personal mission statement. This foundation set the stage for discipline, sacrifice and fortitude to revive the shattered seeds of passion. Many, many seasons following that phone call, my life is different, but good.

How fortunate I was to have had the time at the leadership academy to ponder and craft my mission statement. But it was always there within me. I simply had the time and encouragement to put it into words. Not everyone has a retreat opportunity, but the lack of such an opportunity does not mean the process is not available. The retreat is not as important as the process of introspection. Sometimes that takes place as we are or listening to our favorite music, going for a run or riding a motorcycle. Taking what we learn during our introspection and putting it into words is powerful. Writing it down cements it and grounds us.

There are helpful tools to begin this journey of self discovery. A quick search of the Internet reveals numerous sites that provide guidelines, templates and examples. Ultimately, it is a very personal process and there is no one right way to go about it. Most tools recommend some combination of relaxed brainstorming, reflecting on current roles and identity, naming people of influence in your life, drafting, rewriting…and taking the time.

Once we have put into words what we likely already know, keeping those words close and reviewing them make our personal mission statement a dynamic force in our lives. At home, I keep mine in a drawer next to my bed. At work, I keep it in my planning portfolio. Although I know it by heart, I often take it out and ponder it. Twice a year, New Year's Day and my birthday, I use my personal mission statement as part of a formal personal reflection process. Goals are checked off or modified. Related activities are planned. All fuel my passion, and a new energy emerges. But my personal mission statement remains the same.

A personal mission statement provides guidance when we are faced with a difficult decision. It provides stability in chaos. It provides direction when the way is unclear. It prompts discipline, sacrifice, fortitude and strong character. It creates the right conditions for living passionately.

About the author:

Gwen Koehler is a retired college dean with over thirty-six years of experience in education working with students from middle school through adulthood. Her most challenging work was teaching in a county jail and youth detention center. She has had the privilege to witness the power that education has to transform lives.

She is currently an educational consultant and is pursuing her writing career. She can be reached at gkoehler74@gmail.com.

It Is Never Too Late To Know What You Want To Do When You Grow Up

By Joyce Feustel

MY PASSION IS HELPING OTHER PEOPLE BETTER UNDERSTAND SOCIAL MEDIA

What passion means to me is having an enthusiasm and delight in an activity. When I am passionate about something, time seems to stand still and I feel that I am on the same wavelength as the person I am helping.

As an extrovert and a person devoted to serving others, most of my passionate experiences involve engaging with others and helping them to grow personally, professionally and/or spiritually. I do not have to be physically present with someone to experience passion in helping them. A meaningful connection over a phone call or sometimes through email or social media can also exemplify a passionate encounter with that person.

In the fall of 2010 I started offering social media tutoring services. Although I have been passionate about many things in my life such as my family, being part of Toastmasters, serving in political office and many more, I found myself more passionate about social media tutoring than I have been about any job I have held in my various careers.

It is the transformation in people's experience with social media that keeps me focused on my passion of providing social media tutoring services. What I find the most rewarding is seeing that "aha" look in my client's eyes right in the middle of a tutoring session. Sometimes what they have grasped may seem simple to someone else, but it was not so simple for my client. Once they grasp one aspect of social media, then they often go on to grasp the next concept more easily.

My passion is also ignited when I get that same kind of "aha" look from a student in a social media class. Witnessing the dynamic of classmates in a social media class sharing ideas and challenging me to think outside of the typical social media box also fuels my passion.

WHY IS PASSION IMPORTANT

Countless books have been written on this topic and you will find a number of them in my personal library. They have titles like: *Keep Your Paycheck, Live Your Passion* by Erika Prafder; *Don't Retire, Rewire!* By Jeri Sedlar and Rick Miners; *The Art of the Start* by Guy Kawasaki; *Revive your Drive* by Ken Allen-David and *The Start-Up of You* by Reid Hoffman and Ben Casnocha. Obviously, people are passionate about the topic of passion! They certainly have spent plenty of money on books on this topic.

When I searched in Google and type the phrase: "why passion is important," the first listing I found was an article by Siobhan Harmer posted on the lifehack.org blog. In a thought provoking piece, *10 Reasons Why Following Your Passion is More Important than Money*, Harmer asserts:

"Because you are passionate about what you do, you feel unstoppable and nothing can obstruct you from achieving greatness. Your passion ignites your work, and like a rocket, it accelerates you past roadblocks that may come about. Any obstacle that comes your way is accepted and fought off with a creative solution."

HOW TO FIND YOUR PASSION

Since identifying one's passion is such a personal and often private journey, it is difficult to make broad generalizations on this topic. What I can do is speak for myself in terms of how I found the various passions in my life. Almost every single time I found something I was passionate about, it was because I listened to someone's suggestion and took them up on it.

A friend of mine thought the League of Women Voters would be a great organization for me due to my interest in public policy. She told me when and where the next League meeting was taking place, so I attended and joined. That decision resulted in nearly two decades of active involvement in that organization and I am still a member over 40 years after I joined.

My County Board representative came to me and encouraged me to run for his position, as he had decided not to seek re-election. I had considered running for office someday, but was not sure I was ready. He believed I was ready to serve in that role and nudged me to run. So I took his advice and went on to serve in local elected office.

After meeting with the membership director of a nearby Chamber of Commerce to learn more about working for a chamber, she offered me a position as a membership representative. I had never once thought of going into that line of work. She saw the sales potential in me and offered me a position as a membership representative, aka salesperson, for the Chamber. I went on to work in that field for nearly 17 years.

Shortly after I started working with the Chamber of Commerce, I attended a luncheon where the presenter stressed the importance of public speaking for people who own their own business. He went on to suggest that people who are business owners can learn to be better speakers by joining a local Toastmasters club.

It occurred to me that working in a sales capacity was similar to having my own business. So I sought out the closest Toastmasters club and joined it right away. That was back in 1997 and I am still learning and growing through my Toastmasters participation.

My manager in my most recent sales position noted that I was pretty savvy with social media. He went on to ask me if I had ever thought of helping others to get more comfortable using social media. That idea hadn't crossed my mind until he brought it up.

Because of his observation and comments, I started my social media tutoring business.

Joyce's Back Story

Remember when you were a kid and people would ask you: What do you want to do when you grow up? Growing up as a girl in the 1950s and 1960s, the career options typically offered to me were teaching and nursing. Since my mother had been a teacher, as had several other relatives, I decided to be a teacher too. Yet after two degrees in education and two short stints in the classroom, I discovered that the structured environment of public school teaching just didn't mesh with my rather unstructured spirit.

After exploring work in both the public sector as a public information officer and in the nonprofit sector as the executive director of a nonprofit organization, I still was not any closer to finding a career that made sense to me. Then in December of 1980 I gave birth to my first daughter and in May 1984 to my second daughter. For a time motherhood gave me a respite from career contemplation as I focused on raising my two young girls.

When the girls were 11 and 14 we moved from Madison, Wisconsin to Denver, Colorado. While working in a customer service position, I decided it was time for me to get more career counseling to help me get clarity on where to go with my professional career.

As I was doing informational interviewing as part of my career exploration process, I met with a membership director at a local Chamber of Commerce. I accepted that position and spent the next 17 years in a variety of sales or sales management positions. But had I truly found a "career?"

Though I was proud to call myself a sales professional, I still had not found my passion in my "day jobs." Instead I found it in the speaking and leadership opportunities provided me through my involvement in Toastmasters, an international communication and leadership organization.

However, I still dreamed of a time where I would be able to marry my passion with my career. Part of the dream also included being paid for my services. It was through my involvement with social media that the course of my life would change and my dreams would come true.

SEED OF A BUSINESS IDEA TAKES ROOT

It was through two different friends that I discovered Facebook and LinkedIn in late 2008 right before my 60th birthday. Once I got my arms wrapped around these amazing social media sites, I was hooked! There was something almost magical about being able to connect via LinkedIn with Toastmasters from all over the world and via Facebook with friends and family members, many of whom I rarely get to see.

About a year later, the college where I worked in enrollment launched a Facebook page, LinkedIn group and Twitter account. So, when my manager asked everyone on our team to help promote the college's presence on social media, I quickly started talking up these social media sites with the students who I enrolled into our programs.

Shortly after the social media initiative launched, my manager thanked me for being such an enthusiastic promoter of the college's social media sites. He then asked me if I had ever considered helping other people in my generation to learn about how to use social media.

His words echoed in my head the rest of the day and on the drive home. As much as I enjoyed using social media, it had never occurred to me to help others to get comfortable using social media.

Just as that membership director at the Chamber of Commerce saw the sales potential in me, my current manager saw my potential to be a social media tutor. Sometimes it takes someone else to help us discover our true talents and gifts. I will be forever grateful to my manager for planting the seed for the business I have today.

Fledgling Days of My Business

It takes courage to start a business. I know this very well, as I had started a business back in the early 1990's when my girls were in elementary school. The business consisted of offering research, writing and editing services to local governments, Chambers of Commerce and similar entities. Some years the business made a profit. Some years it did not. Finally, I gave up on it and took an administrative position at my church.

Now here I was with another business concept in front of me - starting a social media tutoring business. For the rest of the spring and all summer I mulled over the pros and cons of following up that idea that my manager had so casually suggested. Finally in the fall of 2010, I decided to go for it. I named my business "Boomers' Social Media Tutor," and I started offering tutoring services to help people get more comfortable with Facebook and LinkedIn.

At first I offered the services on a complimentary basis, just to test out my abilities as a social media tutor and to see if others would benefit from what I offered them. Client by client and month by month, I continued with this self-imposed internship. Time after time, I would see my client's eyes light up as they had their "aha" moments with social media. They were so grateful to me for helping them to have a better grasp of these important communication tools.

After nearly a year of tutoring others on a pro bono basis, I felt I was ready to officially launch my business. I knew that before I did much networking, I would need to have a website for my company. After a few false starts and a web designer who needed to bow out, I found just the right web designer.

My website launched in the spring of 2012, as did my Facebook business page and my blog. Now things were starting to feel real. I even got active on Twitter, which I had been avoiding and was delighted to find Pinterest. So by the summer of 2012 I was getting pretty familiar with four of the major social media sites.

DECIDING WHEN TO LEAVE MY DAY JOB

As passionate as I was about rolling out my services as a social media tutor, I was not quite ready to leave my enrollment position at the college where I worked. I found that work very rewarding, and I was making the most money I had ever made in my life.

Yet between the hours I put in at work, an exhausting commute and my continuing involvement with Toastmasters, it was difficult to devote much time to my business. Trying to do too much, I became so stressed in the fall of 2012 that I developed a respiratory infection that lingered for months.

In late January, just after I turned 64, I saw another career counselor. This time I did not need to take any career aptitude tests or do any informational interviewing. Instead I needed her support as I talked through when to leave the job that I loved for a business that I loved more. Many tears were shed at that session and I will be forever grateful for the support and insight she shared with me that fateful day.

I went to my manager the next day and told him that I planned to retire from my job on March 15. Being someone who does not like abrupt endings, it helped to have just over six weeks to wrap things up with my job at the college.

BECOMING A FULL TIME SOCIAL MEDIA TUTOR

I believe that my training as an educator, the listening and coaching skills I had honed in Toastmasters, and my sales experience all contribute to the success I have today as a social media tutor. Everything we do in life builds on what we have already learned and accomplished.

Yet, even when we are clear on our passion, there are still the dishes to be done, the trash to take out and the dogs to be walked. If a passion is done through a business, such as mine is, there are still the networking groups to attend, books to be balanced and appointments to be set.

Very few of us are truly in the groove of our passion during most of our waking time. Other activities need to be done so that we have the chance as much as possible to be living our passion.

However, if I did not love what I do in terms of helping people truly embrace and use social media, it would be much more difficult to do all the footwork that goes into setting up the client appointments and planning for the classes I teach. Having passion for something is critical in order to maintain the stamina and energy to create a foundation on which the passion-filled activities take place.

About the author:

Joyce Feustel founded Boomers' Social Media Tutor in 2012. She provides personalized social media tutoring and social media training to people new, or relatively new, to such social media websites as Facebook, LinkedIn, Twitter, Pinterest and others.

She works with job seekers, business owners, retired people and leaders of nonprofit groups to help them become more proficient with social media. A graduate of the University of Wisconsin – Madison, Joyce has worked in education and business.

Hearts for Haiti

By Gene Seaver

I traveled to several countries in Europe, the Czech Republic and Slovakia, after Russia released their political power and control over the countries in Eastern and Central Europe. Renewal Ministries of Ann Arbor, Michigan felt a need to reach out to the people of these former communist controlled countries and began sending Evangelization teams to Europe. My first mission was to Presov, Slovakia and then on future missions to include the Czech Republic.

Upon returning from one of my mission trips, my wife very seriously looked at me and said, "The Lord is calling you to go to Africa." Going to Africa was never a desire of mine and my reply was at first laughter then firm verbal, "No way. I'm not going to Africa." However I learned that the county coordinator was Tom Edwards, the same man who was the leader of the missions to Slovakia and the Czech Republic. A mission was planned for the month of January to Tanzania, a country in East Africa.

I can't explain it but the word Tanzania kept flowing through my mind constantly. Finally I said, "OK Lord. If this is what you want me to do, I will go." I then emailed Tom and very apologetically offered to be on the team if he had room for me thinking that the team was already full since I was replying at such a late date. To my surprise I immediately received a reply, "Your on the team."

After receiving information about this mission I was told that another team would continue on to the country of Kenya and I was welcomed to join them if I desired. At this time I only had my visa to Tanzania but not Kenya. The date was very late but if I hurried and sent my passport express mail I could still get the visa on time. Unknown to me, the staff at the Kenyan Embassy was on Christmas break and no one was there to process my visa. My family and I were frantic. Not only did I not have the visa for Kenya but also they had my passport and my flight was scheduled to leave in four days. I began to believe that this was a message from my Lord that I was not to go to Africa.

My daughters intervened and began calling the embassy. They were able to have my passport and visa shipped by overnight express mail. I received my passport on Saturday and my flight was on Sunday so now I was totally convinced that my Lord truly wanted me to go to Africa.

I have read about Africa, saw movies depicting life in Africa, but to be there and to experience it first hand gave me a knowledge and awareness of the culture and living conditions of these people I never had before. I believe now that this experience was meant to prepare me for Haiti.

I joined the team from my church, the Church of Holy Apostles in McHenry, Illinois, to go on a mission to Haiti. In Haiti, at the compound of the Sisters of Charity, The sisters of Mother Teresa, wherever a crucifix is placed on a wall there also was the phrase placed next to it, "I Thirst." What a Blessing for us to pray with the Sisters of Charity! What a Blessing to attend Mass with them and to attend Eucharist adoration with them! What a blessing to be part of the ministry of caring for the children during the day!

As we prayed with the sisters in their Chapel, I looked at the Crucifix behind the altar and the words next to it, "I Thirst," and meditated on the meaning of these words. It is a new life for all of us now, a life we did not know before or understand. It is a new awakening; a truth and reality of life in Haiti with the poorest of the poor. I meditated on how much of the world is in similar poverty and I meditated how much Jesus thirsts for souls in Haiti, America and the world.

Jesus asked the woman at the well, to her surprise, "Give me a drink." Later in the Gospel of John 19:28, Jesus said while hanging on the cross, "I Thirst." Reflecting on the spiritual meaning of the words of Jesus, he is saying that he is thirsting for souls. My understanding, as I thought about these words, is that God is bringing me to these various situations and places, surrounded by many people, because they are the souls He is seeking and thirsting for. Somehow I am part of bringing these souls to Christ through my words and actions. I am overwhelmed with awe with the opportunity God has given me.

We are a group of nine people who agreed to go to Haiti to serve people in the poorest country in the western hemisphere. Our quarters are within the compound of the Sisters of Charity in a concrete block building called the guest house. It is located at the far end of the property, off by itself, near to the orphanage and medical center. Provided in the lower level is a kitchen for all the volunteers. It has a propane fueled gas stove, a microwave oven and a small refrigerator. Every day, different members of the team prepared meals according to a prearranged schedule.

Each day we worked with and helped the sisters at the children's clinic and orphanage. They preferred not to call it a hospital even though people would bring sick and dying and abandoned babies and children to be cared for by the sisters in the hope their lives would be saved.

The medical center and orphanage is a simple place without any extravagance. It consisted of rooms with cribs, about twenty per room. The children were separated; it seemed, according to the degree of illness except for one room, which was for very small babies. Some children were lying down, some were standing and some were outside their cribs walking around. Occasionally some older children were outside playing in the courtyard. Very few toys could be seen; a few here and there brought in by some volunteer. I brought two stuffed dolls that were quickly snatched up outside as I approached through the play area to the building. The children didn't seem to know how to play with toys or understand what they were for. The few toys available to them were only something to possess, as they had nothing.

It was sad to see children who were very malnourished and extremely thin, skin and bones, and often lethargic as a result of little or no food for an extended period of time before being brought to the Sisters of Charity. While we were there, babies were brought in that aged from one and a half to two years old that weighted only six pounds. With nutritional food and medical care they often recovered very quickly. However, some could not be saved and died because they were too sick, malnourished and weak to survive. Babies who had been abandoned and not brought in soon enough, died from lack of food and illness. With each of my trips to this facility babies had died.

One wonders, in a country so poor and because of disease from impure water, suffering from tuberculosis and AIDS, lack of food children and adults are dying; what could be done individually or collectively to improve conditions and raise the living standard of the people. What could we do to help them improve their situation?

We knew that we could bring things that were needed in our luggage. Because the flight was considered international, we were allowed to bring two fifty-pound pieces of luggage and also a carry-on bag that conforms to size limitation. We brought more than twelve hundred pounds of medical supplies, clothing and school supplies for the children and adults in the area. Everything we brought was very much appreciated, especially the medicine and hospital supplies.

Each day began with Mass with the sisters. The Chapel was a small room with a thin carpet on the floor. There were no pews or chairs except a few along the back wall for some visitors. The sisters would kneel and we, the volunteers behind them would imitate the sisters as best we could. I could not help but observe the sisters during Mass. It was like being in a room full of angels or more accurately, saints. The presence of God was so strong that love seemed to radiate from everyone. We joined the sisters in the prayers and singing during Mass and also after Mass.

Shoes were not allowed in the Chapel so the sisters and most people were bare footed. A few children would join us each morning and they too were bare footed. Although very young, the children displayed a piety not often seen of children of that age. As I felt my own bare feet touch the floor of this holy place I immediately sensed I was truly very much part of it, part of what was happening in that room. I became aware of an interesting sensation because of being bare footed with the others in the Chapel. As I looked forward and saw the bare feet of the sisters and knew my feet, my skin, touched where they had walked; I felt a oneness with everyone there as we gave ourselves to God in the Mass and received the flesh and blood of Jesus with His soul and divinity in the Eucharist.

The first day I was interested in what the priest, Father Tom, would say during the homily to these holy women of God. I learned so much that first day and the subsequent days about the truth of life, of our relationship to God and to each other. On that first day, Father Tom talked about the relationship of our flesh and our souls and the relationship of the combination of our flesh and souls to God.

Now I understand more deeply the concept of the body being the temple of the soul and the soul the temple of the Holy Spirit and how the body is to serve the soul as the soul serves God. The body is not to serve and adore itself and thereby cause the soul to turn away from God to serve the body. The Beatitudes are more understandable now along with a detachment from earthly goods. Our souls are to focus on the love of God in all things we do regardless of the circumstances. Through Father Tom we learned a child in the slums was shot in the head by a gang. He was very concerned about the seriousness of her injuries and asked that we pray for her. Before we returned home from our mission Father Tom told us she was doing well and would recover.

As we left the Chapel that first morning we stood around talking, not wanting to leave but to remain a bit longer immersed in God's love and peace. We put on our shoes that were along the outside wall and slowly walked back to the guest house to take care of our personal needs and to eat breakfast. Our scheduled time to begin with the children was not until eight AM.

The guest house was very nice compared to what we had seen on our way from the airport. Although we did not have electrical power at night, the kerosene lamps gave plenty of light for our needs and for reading. We had no TV, radio, phones, etc. to distract us. We felt no stress or anxiety concerning the problems of the world, as we did not have any news of events outside of our compound. A comment was stated of how peaceful it felt and how nice it is not to worry about things we have no power over. By this time our group had bonded and we were truly a team.

Everyone had begun their work as though they had been there before. The team began doing different tasks in various rooms as was needed and according to individual skills. All of us fed, changed soiled clothing and diapers and played with the children. Those skilled medically assisted with IVs and injections. The children were begging to be selected for our attention and to be picked up, hugged, loved and comforted. They would cry and wail until someone would come to them. Some children were too sick to cry but in their eyes we could see their pleading for some love from us. We attended to as many children as possible and at times with three or four at once.

It occurred to me how needy mankind is for God and his love and how we cry and wail to him constantly for his attention. Some of us are too spiritually sick to cry and wail for God's attention and love. Yet God is always comforting, feeding and caring for our needs and most of all he is giving us his unconditional love.

It was evident as I held a child in my arms that God was really the one who was holding him. I had such a wonderful degree of contentment because it was God that was loving and holding these babies with my arms. My body was serving the soul as the soul was serving God through loving the child I was holding. This was similar to the Chapel experience that in holding one of the least and giving love to the poorest of the poor, the weak and the dying; the presence of God was felt in a very strong way.

The children were so delighted with the attention we gave them. Their faces were filled with joy and happiness throughout the time we were allowed to be with them. Between the hours of 12 noon to 3 p.m. the children were kept quiet for rest and we returned back to our quarters during that time. We then had our noon meal and also rested or read. Some of us took this time to go out for supplies and food. There was opportunity to talk and share our experiences. Everyone had a great story to share of their ministering to the children.

After our supper meal we went to the Chapel for an hour of Adoration with the sisters. An hour of thanksgiving and praise followed our day's work and we thanked our Lord for his grace in allowing us to be so much an integral part of his work. We are so happy to have the opportunity to work in the medical center and orphanage and experience the children throughout the day and giving of ourselves as was needed. We spoke to Jesus, present in the Eucharist, of the beautiful moments we had that day. We sang, we prayed and we adored our Lord. As a team we also prayed the Divine Office prayer each evening with the sisters.

At the guest house lanterns were lit as the sun went down in the evening and flashlights were used to light the area in our rooms. A simple retreat was presented before we retired for the night. The retreat helped us to focus in a spiritual direction. The first night we talked about love, a new commandment that Jesus gave us, "Love one another as I have loved you." Love must accompany all that we do each day. The love Jesus commands us to give is the love He gives to us.

The second night we spoke about repentance, how necessary it is for us to be willing to change our lives, to turn away from the world and draw closer to God; to begin a new life of putting God first in everything.

The third evening we learned about the dangers of temptation and listened to the Words of our Lord in that we are to serve and worship God alone. We learned to constantly pray for the strength to overcome temptation.

The forth night was lesson on the Sermon on the Mount beginning with the Beatitudes and the need to change our attitude with a better understanding of the Beatitudes. We were told we must live the Beatitudes, not just some of them but all of them as they are the stepping stones to heaven.

The last and final night of our stay in Haiti we addressed the joy of living in the presence of God as we served Him and the children with the sisters. It was acknowledged by all of the team that there was so much joy in all that we were exposed to by the knowledge that we gave everything to our Lord these few days and because of our giving everything for the honor and glory of God, this is the source of our joy.

Our scheduled time went very fast. We arrived on Monday with great eagerness to begin our mission and now at the end of this last day, Friday, we were sad as we began to prepare for our early departure the next day. Plans were already being made for our return for another mission.

All of us learned many important lessons of life. One lesson that I learned was that material things did not bring true happiness. Loving and serving God by giving ourselves to God's children gave more happiness then all the material possessions that we have. Another lesson for me was that the poor of Haiti found a deeper meaning in life as they helped each other day to day to just survive. They appeared not to look so much to tomorrow, but were interested in what was needed just for today. The poor need each other and they have a deep thirst for God and in their poverty they know God thirsts for them. Only with the grace of God will they survive.

Now as I reflect back on my experience of this week in Haiti I feel a deeper understanding of the meaning of the words of Jesus, "I Thirst." Jesus thirsts for all of us and He is asking us to thirst for Him. To thirst for Jesus is to be obedient to Him and to Our Father in all things, to always put God first in all we do. It means to serve those around us whether poor in material possessions or poor in faith and understanding of God. We are called to serve every one with the gifts we were given.

The team now has been given the grace to know and understand more of the meaning of life. We exist to know God, to love God, to serve Him and those He puts in our life's path with the expectation of everlasting life. This team and the other teams all understand now that wherever God calls us to go, we will go, and whatever God calls us to do, we will do. To be part of Jesus' calling out to us personally from the cross, "I Thirst" and to be given the grace to respond is truly a blessing and a joy.

About the author:

Gene Seaver enjoys retirement and spending time with his close family. He has been married for 57 years to his wife Patricia and they have seven children and 23 grandchildren. While owner and operator of Eagle Commercial Refrigeration Service he is active in his church including missionary trips throughout the world. You can learn more about supporting missionaries and people in need by visiting CatholicAssistanceMissions.org and www.renewalministries.net. You can contact Gene at geneseaver@wonderwave.net.

Importance of Understanding Your Passion and How to Find Your Passion

By Linda Hayes

WHAT AM I PASSIONATE ABOUT?

Passion for a specific thing changes with every chapter we live in our lives. What we were passionate about yesterday may not be what we are passionate about today. Why is this? Are we fickle and shallow? No, we are not. In fact as we move through life we find areas that we want to throw our entire mind and heart into, to master and expand our life and world. Once we have accomplished that goal it is time to grow again as we find another area to discover and master through our passionate endeavors.

However, each of us has a deeper life purpose that propels us forward through each life experience we master passionately. What I am referring to is the core essence of our heart and soul. When I look back on my life I notice a pattern. This pattern may not be so very clear to me at times but it is a pattern nonetheless. I have spent my life giving to others and developing the qualities of compassion, kindness, and endurance. I am known as a compassionate woman with a kind giving heart. Sometimes this pattern is more obvious. Each and every goal I have achieved has had this underlying core value of compassion, kindness, and endurance as the foundation.

For example, I was a strong outspoken twenty year old rebel in Oakland in the 70's fighting for peace and equality. Later in life I successfully nurtured five children as a single mother devoting every waking moment to them. I had to develop strong compassion to keep my heart from hatred as I looked back over a nineteen year abusive marriage to an alcoholic husband. Years have passed yet I still hold onto the same desire to be compassionate to others and help them through their life trials by teaching them endurance and reliance on God. This is my core essence that influences each endeavor I pursue with deep passion.

I remember the words of my oldest son when he was still a teenager. We were being evicted for the third time in eighteen months. My children ranged in age from four to sixteen. My husband had not paid the rent again. As we were packing up our things before we made our great escape from my husband my son said, "You should leave him a box, a plate, and silverware and nothing else. He has taken us through hell."

I told him, "No, I refuse to let anyone take away my good heart and my compassionate spirit. I cherish those traits and that is who I am."

People say that I have lived a life full of situations that others will never experience. I was estranged from my birth family for over twenty years. When I finally made amends I discovered that my mother was deep into Alzheimer's disease. She would never be able to hear my words of sorrow and my apology to her for hanging onto a twenty year old fight with her. When I finally saw my favorite brother again after twenty years he died within a week with me at his side. The grief I felt was deep because I had let time and indifference rob us of our relationship. Some experiences have been heart breaking and very hard. But I believe that everything I have struggled with in life was for a reason. Each struggle has strengthened my core essence of compassion, kindness, and endurance. Each lesson learned from my experiences are lessons I can share with others to help them.

How then have I manifested my core essence? My passion is to be transparent and honest with others as I speak about my life struggles. My passion is to take my struggles and success stories and encourage others to turn their heartaches into success stories too. My passion is to use my stories to help heal the hearts of others. I have been given the gift of compassion, kindness, and endurance and I will use this gift to help people overcome adversity.

How Did I Find My Passion?

I spent years carrying out the roles I played in life such as wife and mother. My waking hours were filled with protecting my children from harm, filtering the sadness of a dysfunctional home life and providing for their needs. There was little time to think about my passions or myself. I lived out my passion without thinking about what it was, what to do with it, or how to develop it. Compassion, endurance and deep family love motivated my daily activities. Deep faith in God's protection and wisdom carried me along with each life stage I encountered. My passion was to nurture my family and help them to succeed.

When I finally became successful according to the world's barometer I had time to reflect on what I was meant to do. The puzzle pieces of my life and my core essence qualities now fit together. Struggling to raise my family and be a responsible parent no longer dominated by waking thoughts. It was now time to take a look at me. I had become a successful Director of a district wide K-12 food program. I was responsible for 36,000 students, 220 staff members and 40 site kitchens.

This seeming success was not what excited me. On the contrary, I realized that I had the power to create change for children. I remembered my five children feeling inferior as they received their free lunches at school in designated areas for free meals. Before long they stopped eating at school because they were embarrassed. I felt a strong drive to make a difference with the position I had been given. My passion grew and exploded as I created a meal program that made each and every student feel good about eating with us. No student would be singled out for being poor and receiving free meals.

I jumped in and created food courts to please the eyes of the students. Colorful themed eating areas with decorations and fancy serving baskets became our norm in the school kitchens. The separate meal lines for the free students were eliminated. The exchange of cash was minimized as I replaced our lucrative a la carte program with complete meals for all students. Some of my peers thought I was crazy and irresponsible for converting a lucrative sales program into a program for the betterment of our kids. I discovered that the twinge of sadness and emotion I felt in my heart when I talked about needy kids was my growing passion to change the world and let my core essence of compassion, kindness, and endurance shine brightly.

My passion for change paid off. My program was very successful for our students and financially for our program. We became pioneers in a new student oriented meal program that was copied by other districts in the years that followed. Now as I mentioned earlier, the manifestation of our core essence as seen through our endeavors and accomplishments changes with each chapter of life we experience. I found that I no longer had the deep passion for what I was doing. I had accomplished what I set out to do. I became discontent and unsure of what new path to take in the future. What I did know was that something else would captivate my attention and create the passion I had lost.

I prayed intently for light and wisdom to show me what I should do next. During this time I had embarked on a new endeavor to share my life story with others. I had been working on my book for four years and had 75 pages. My first manuscript was more of a journal than a book.

One day I felt that funny sad and emotional twinge in my heart. It was time to take a new leap forward. I threw myself into rewriting my story and wrote every waking moment I could spare. I wrote on my lunch breaks, evenings, and weekends. Within six months my book was birthed containing the secrets I had held back for decades. My deep passion was to tell my story to the world, to share my defeats and success stories, and to help each reader heal their hearts and find joy.

I am now a transformational author. The words I pen are meant to transform peoples' lives. I can feel this deep desire running through my entire mind, body, and spirit. I have now been able to integrate my core essence of compassion, kindness, and endurance as I fulfill my destiny and life path fully. My passion has become me and I am now finally free to be me.

HOW CAN YOU FIND YOUR PASSION?
- First put all your predefined ideas of the meaning of passion to the side. Instead look inside yourself. Find the deep feelings that you cherish about life, family, and others. *Identify these feelings.*
- Next think about the things that were important to you as a child, the heartfelt qualities that were a natural part of your spirit. *Identify these qualities and find your core essence.* You will know if the qualities you identify are your core traits by the way they make you feel. They will feel natural and comfortable. People will say that you have these qualities. For example, people always say that I am kind, loving, compassionate and giving. I am known for these traits and I feel comfortable practicing them.
- Think about each chapter of your life. How did those experiences mold you into who you are today? *Identify how your core essence qualities were part of those experiences. Identify the passion you felt during those life chapters.* The passion you felt does not have to be goal oriented all the time. As a matter of fact passion can be found in wholeheartedly caring for tasks like raising a family or studying in school.
- Look at your life today. Are you missing something? Do you feel complacent or unfulfilled? Are you plodding along existing rather than finding excitement in your life? *Reignite your core essence qualities of your heart.* You can do this by honest self-evaluation your life. If you feel stuck in a rut then change what you are doing. Begin adding new things into your life a little at a time. Bring back some of the things you love to do and develop them more fully. When you do this passion will grow in your life.

Once you have evaluated your present state jump in wholeheartedly and passionately. You may have to take a leap of faith, change your comfort zone, change direction or fine tune what you are doing. You will know if you are on the right path because you will feel it in our heart and the passion will become so strong that you will be not be able to ignore it anymore.

A few days ago I was talking to fellow author and friend. I had been going through a slump and not only had no passion but I had no desire to do anything. She asked me what I envisioned as my career. I told her "I am an author. I am also a motivational speaker." I felt that I really did not know what to talk about so I was stuck, running in place. How could I fit my life experiences into the corporate world to make some money? When I told her this she laughed.

"Linda, it is quite simple you are a writer. Your book transforms lives and you want to talk about your book. Your audience is not the corporate world; you are trying to fit a square peg into a round hole!" Her words made sense and I marveled as I thought of the many months I had been overcome with confusion. "Linda, you are a transformational author. You write to transform lives." As soon as I heard the title it felt right. The words were melodic to my ears and it was comfortable.

Once you identify what you want to do and set a plan of action. You will know if it is right because the idea and words will resonate in you and make you feel great. There will be no doubt in your mind that you found your passion and want to pursue it wholeheartedly.

- Last step: *Jump in, do it, follow your dream.* Do not let other people's opinions sway you from manifesting passion in your life! Stay true to yourself and your dreams and you will succeed.

About the author:

Linda Hayes was born in Southern California to first generation immigrants from the Philippines. She grew up in the Philippines and attended college in the United States. Her life as a mother of five children trapped in poverty with an abusive alcoholic husband for 19 years changed when she recaptured the rebel spirit of her youth and ended her marriage. She has turned oppressive circumstances into building blocks for success.

She is a successful businesswoman, a transformational author and speaker. She encourages changing obstacles into success stories. She authored *The Voice Hidden Within Me - A Journey of Discovery and Healing Your Heart* and her new upcoming cookbook *Simply Tasty-Easy Meals on a Budget*. You can visit her at: www.HeartChatter.com and www.Publishing-USA.com. Books are available at www.amazon.com/dp/0988545306. See her author page at www.amazon.com/author/lindahayes.

It's Never Too Late!

By Joyce Kocinski

What are your talents and dreams? What do you hope to accomplish in the next few years? Are you waiting to start a course or take a class because you aren't sure it's the right time for you? What is holding you back from starting a new career or new job?

These are the questions you need to ask yourself when discovering and following your passion(s) in life. I say, "passions" as we all have various strengths and interests that, over time, can develop to help us succeed in our careers. What job you start in your twenties may not be the same career in your thirties or forties.

I always knew I wanted to be a teacher since childhood so I earned my Bachelor degree in Elementary Education with a minor in special education right out of college. Thirty years ago teaching mentally challenged students in private schools was difficult to say the least. The two private schools where I taught had no curriculum and I had to develop one myself. The class was a mix of nonverbal and mentally challenged students.

I soon became burned out, as there was no set curriculum. I took a job at a daycare center to work with two year olds. They have so much energy and enthusiasm at that age. Little did I know that being a teacher would always figure into my life plans and I would be back teaching students with disabilities in the future.

After a few years, I took some time off from teaching and entered the business world with an insurance company. My life was in transition as I was trying to decide whether to leave the teaching field (half my fellow employees at the company were ex-teachers!) As a contract analyst, I wrote copy for the insurance booklets employers passed out to their employees. Two years later, I took a promotion as an underwriter. Soon, I met my husband, married and left the company when I was expecting my first child. I enjoyed being a "stay at home" mom, but when my daughter turned two years old, I went back to teaching at a day-care center. That way while she was in a different classroom, I could still exercise my talent for teaching and contribute to the family income. Teaching preschool age children also helped me learn how to be a more educated parent.

Something was missing in my life. I had artistic talent and loved to draw as a child as my mother had always encouraged my talent. In my thirties, I took an oil painting class. My daughter was still young so I did painting workshops on the weekends. It felt good to make time for my hobby. After several classes, I joined two art leagues and displayed my work at their shows. Besides selling artwork, I gave some paintings away as gifts to my family and friends. My specialty was landscapes and seascapes until I saw a floral artist doing an exhibit. Then I fell in love with painting flowers: roses, iris and lilacs. I developed my skills and even did some commissions for clients. Art became my new hobby and passion in my life.

Do you have a hobby you use to do when you were young and have put it off for some reason? Make the time to start it up again, and see how relaxed you will be when you are following your passion. When I started oil painting, time flew by and a four hour workshop went by quickly. You become lost in the moment with the power to create something beautiful.

When you take a class or a hobby and explore your passion, it doesn't have to be a moneymaking hobby. Do it for the enjoyment and if you happen to make some money, congratulations! Making money should not be the goal or you may become frustrated. You do not need to hold yourself to a strict schedule. The point is we all have talents or strengths and only need the motivation to start. Maybe you used to write poetry, draw or sketch for fun, it doesn't matter. The point is you are taking time for yourself and will feel better for it.

One of my life long interests is family history. Years ago, I started interviewing my parents and recorded their memories of names and dates of family trees ultimately doing the research to back up my work. I sent away for birth and death certificates before records were computerized and collected numerous documents on both sides of the tree. Over time, I gathered photos and put together chronological notebooks. Working on family history is like being a detective. You find facts on some documents that lead you to other areas. Sometimes name of towns are misspelled and that leads you to contact more sources. Eventually you may find branches of your family tree and other relatives interested in the same quest. I corresponded with relatives in Poland and then actually got to meet them on a trip and tour of the country several years ago.

Whatever your interest, it's never too late to pick it up again and follow its lead. You might meet others interested in the same hobby and start a new friendship. Maybe you have more than one hobby or interest that you can pick up and try again. Besides art, writing is one of my passions. It was an outlet for me ever since high school, after I wrote an article for the school newspaper. The reaction I got from students and teachers alike was enough to validate my talent. I made an impression on some of the teachers with my editorial, A Day in the Life. Synopsis: a student goes through her day at school afraid to speak up if she doesn't understand because she does not want the teacher to respond in a negative way or have other students make fun of her. When a teacher asks if there are any questions and no one responds, she assumes everyone knew the work. It was apparent that it touched some teachers as a few actually asked me if the teacher in the article was one of them!

Writing in a journal became a way of recording my feelings as well as family events. Releasing emotions through writing in my diary was cathartic and healing. For example, I lived with my grandmother my junior year of college. She lived alone and was house bound, so I enjoyed cooking and cleaning for her. We became close and I was her part time companion even though she spoke Polish and knew very little English. That summer she fell and broke her hip. After staying in the hospital, she was transferred to a nursing home and died six weeks later. After she died, I cried for days but I wrote about her in my diary to keep my memories alive. Writing became more than a hobby. It was my salvation. It kept me sane. I could pick up a journal anytime and work through life changing moments.

One of those moments was deciding on a career change. Over a period of ten years, I worked as a substitute teacher, teacher aid and special education teacher. I went back to school, (thanks to the financial support of my husband) and completed my Master's degree in Education. Somehow, teaching always played a part in my career. However, I still needed to satisfy the creative urge inside of me. I followed my "passion" of helping friends and family redesign their homes. When a friend moved to a new house, I helped her rearrange her living room. Gradually, I did similar work with friends and family members and my confidence grew. I became excited about my new hobby.

Lifelong learning is the result of following your passions. It keeps your creative mind alert and active. When you allow yourself to try new activities, you are bringing new energy into your life.

For example, when I decided to donate teacher and curriculum manuals I no longer used, I was letting go of the past. It felt free. That was the beginning of my decision to go back to school and get my interior design degree. At age 50, I started the program with students half my age. I followed a passion that gave me credibility to the work I was already doing. I wrote a term paper on Feng Shui as a design trend and became enamored of the topic. When I found a teacher in the area, I took her class, became certified in it and added that as one of my design services. The goal of Feng Shui is to increase the positive energy flow in your home. It was no surprise to me that I started getting new design clients and growing in my design career when I did a Feng Shui analysis on my own home. Part of that design process is clearing the physical clutter from your home and office. I bought new file cabinets, organized my papers and started donating items that did not serve a purpose or brought negative energy when I saw it.

Soon I started my own interior design business. Through self-promotion, word of mouth I got new clients. By advertising and contacting the local community college, I developed design workshops and classes I offered to the public. Still the teacher, I enjoy helping people learn the principles of design and was successful at it.

Life went on and I taught interior design classes, combining my love of teaching and design. I branched out and started writing articles for design publications (my other passion, writing!) I worked with the owner of a local furniture store to redesign their displays. One of my biggest supporters in my new career was my mother. She would suggest ideas for design plans, had good taste in color and accessories and gave me praise when I needed it most. She was staying with me while recovering from a broken leg when she had a heart attack. After surgery for her heart condition, she was in and out of hospitals and nursing homes for over a year. I was grateful to be able to spend time with her and even bring my cat, Tiny, to visit her in the rehabilitation home.

When my mother died after a long illness, I started a journal to process my grief. This was a suggestion from the chaplain who ran the grief workshop I took at the local hospital. At first I wrote daily, then it gradually became weekly, then monthly. As I reread my words, I saw the progress I was making dealing with her death. The idea of a book blossomed in my head as I decided to combine the journal and letters I had saved from her over the years. The book was a gift to my family and friends. Thus, at age 60, I wrote and published my first book, *Letters from Mom - a Daughter's Journal of Healing*. This is spiritual book that helped me strengthen my faith in God at a time when I needed it most. Losing a parent is hard enough but when you can share your grief with others, it becomes easier to handle.

Writing that book led to a local writer's group and other fellow writers. I started a blog, *Joyce's Journal*, as my way of sharing my life experiences interlaced with positive messages of hope and inspiration. I make it a point for my essays to be uplifting and informative and sometimes humorous.

Everyone has latent talents that can come out when given the right timing and support. Try the hobby you started when you were young and see where it leads. Perhaps you will find a new pastime in your thirties or forties. As you grow, so do your talents, if given the chance. We have to be open to believing in ourselves and our right to exercise our passions. Faith in God and in my talents has helped me follow my passions throughout my life. I cannot do it alone and neither can you. Find a friend or family member who believes in your passions and supports your efforts. Let your passions carry you through out life and see what develops. Sometimes we cannot guess what the plan for our lives is but must be willing to be open to change. Trust that you have the right to follow your passions and see where it leads!

About the author:

Joyce Kocinski has a Master's degree in education and teaches education and student development courses at Elgin Community College. She is also a degreed interior designer certified in Interior Alignment Feng Shui and gives workshops on various design related topics. She helps clients through her interior design business, Design in Balance www.designinbalance.com. She published her first book, *Letters from Mom - a Daughter's Journal of Healing*, which is available on amazon.com. You can view her blog, *Joyce's Journal* at joycekocinski.wordpress.com or contact her at jkocinski@wowway.com.

A Passion for Flight

By Ed Finnegan

Simply put, my passion is flying. Flying airplanes is what I do as a profession and what I do for enjoyment. It's what I've always wanted to do with my life. I cannot remember a time when I was not looking skyward and wishing that I was up in the air. The air is my natural element; it is where I am most comfortable. I believe that flying is in my DNA. It is what I was born to do.

My earliest childhood memories contain images of me sitting in our large backyard watching airplanes fly overhead. Growing up in western Pennsylvania, my family lived underneath several routes that airliners used between airports on the East coast and airports in the Midwest. My older brother and I kept very detailed records on time of sighting, direction of flight, estimated altitude, and the amount of time during which the airplane was in view. As a youngster, I remember spending hours sitting in the tallest tree in the yard thinking of how great it would be to be able to fly like a bird. I read everything I could about airplanes, especially the airplanes from World War II. I could recite all the performance details of just about all the fighters and bombers from that era. I dreamed of flying those airplanes one day.

As I grew older, I decided that flying was what I would do as my life's occupation. But flying was more than just an occupation or a vocation. It was my passion. It was what I was constantly thinking about. The answer to that question: "What do you want to do when you grow up?" was easy for me. I wanted to fly!

I was blessed with very loving and supportive parents, but my family was of modest means. Money was always tight and there certainly was not any disposable income to be spent on flying lessons for me. I recognized very early in my life that if I wanted something, I was going to have to work for it. I was willing to work hard, but oftentimes hard work is not enough for success. I also knew that I needed a plan. I had my goal, now I had to develop a plan that would facilitate the accomplishment of that goal. And a reality about flying is that it costs money, a lot of money. Looks like I needed to get a job!

I worked at several different jobs while in high school, but my favorite job was working as a line boy at the local airport. I worked evenings and weekends, fueling airplanes and cleaning the offices at night. I enjoyed being around the airplanes and the mechanics and flight instructors. I tried to learn something from them and was always eagerly looking for an opportunity to go flying. I saved my money and spent most of it on flying lessons. I soloed on my 18th birthday and got my license shortly thereafter.

Now for another dose of reality: in order to further my credentials in aviation and to get more ratings on my pilot license meant a lot of flying and a lot of money. Far more money than my meager resources could allow. Perhaps a change in strategy was needed. Another life lesson: keep the goal in sight, but be flexible on how you achieve that goal. I decided to join the military and become a military-trained pilot. I may as well get paid as an officer while I fly. Really? Pay me to fly? Yup! I'm all over that! Additionally, it is good to serve my nation.

After college, I was off to helicopter flight school. My thinking was that a company might want to hire someone who is rated in both helicopters and airplanes. I might be able to command a higher salary if I was rated in both. Qualifying as a United States Army Aviator is difficult. U.S. Army flight school is tough. It should be tough. The demands on the Army Aviator can be extreme. But with the help of my wife, I was able to excel and graduated as the Distinguished Honor Graduate. I was first in my class. Wow! Now I have a choice: Flying the helicopter of my choice anywhere in the world, or fixed-wing reconnaissance airplanes and an assignment to the Republic of Korea. A seemingly tough choice but a very easy answer: OV-1 Mohawks to Korea.

Another lesson: when presented with shiny new temptations, remember the plan…

In my flight class of sixty students, I was granted the only fixed-wing training slot. As a result of learning to fly airplanes the U.S. Army way I stayed at Fort Rucker, Alabama long after all of my classmates had left. After all of my additional training and aircraft transitions, I was off to Fort Huachuca, Arizona, for military intelligence training. The G-OV1 Mohawk was a reconnaissance aircraft, thus we had to learn how to employ it in that role. What a beautiful place! Many people found the desert of southern Arizona to be ugly, but my wife and I found the desert possessed a beauty all its own. Another lesson: natural beauty is all around us. We just have to stop and recognize it. The three months went by so quickly at Fort Huachuca. Now it was time to serve my nation in the capacity for which I had spent so much time training.

My year in the Republic of Korea was unexpectedly enjoyable. My military friends became lifelong friends and I learned how to fly in adverse conditions in a wartime environment. Because the Korean War has never ended, a Cease Fire Agreement, that wasn't always adhered to, maintained the peace. The friendships and the skills learned while flying in Korea have been relevant to me my entire career.

In July 1987, after my year of working all day and flying all night ended, I transferred to another reconnaissance unit in the Federal Republic of Germany. It was the same mission, but a different adversary. Instead of flying east to west along the 38th parallel observing North Korea, was now flying north to south along the German border keeping an eye on activity in East Germany. Again, it was some of the best flying a young aviator could have in his or her career. I was actually on a mission when the East German border was opened and free travel was permitted between the two Germanys. It was very gratifying to be a small part of such historic events. We won the Cold War.

Now for more life lessons: Life is full of choices and know thyself. After three years in Germany, it was time to make a choice. I was very good at being a leader, an officer in the U.S. Army and could have made the Army a career. Many contemporaries thought that I would be a career officer and I did consider it. But flight time is inversely proportional to rank. Which did I love more, the U.S. Army or flying? I was very good at both. I could stay in the U.S. Army and live the life of a military officer, or I could leave all of that behind and take the leap of faith and accept a huge risk and try my luck in the commercial aviation field. I chose aviation. All things aviation had been a part of my life since I could remember and aviation was my true passion. Therefore, I chose to stay focused on my dream and kept working to achieve that dream.

I sent applications to all the airlines in 1990 and I was interviewed and subsequently hired by American Airlines. Part of my dream was realized. I was a professional pilot! I was getting paid (not very much, but it was still a paycheck) to fly airplanes all over the country!

Now on to part two of my dream: flying the airplanes from World War II, simply called "Warbirds."

Since childhood I had heard of an organization based in Wisconsin called the Experimental Aircraft Association (EAA). Originally formed as a group of individuals who built their own airplanes, the organization has expanded to include many different facets of aviation. EAA now includes a division called Warbirds of America (WOA). Warbirds of America's goal is to promote the preservation and presentation of all former military aircraft, commonly called "warbirds." Their motto is, "Keep 'Em Flying!" and they are definitely a group with whom I wish to be associated. So I signed up and began meeting people who were just as enthusiastic and passionate about aviation and old warbirds as I was. And they either knew, or were flying these airplanes themselves!

One handshake and introduction leads to another and now I am on the Board of Directors for EAA Warbirds of America. I am qualified on many different warbirds and fly them on a regular basis. I am also a check airman on several of these airplanes and am authorized to train and evaluate other pilots. I always seem to have an old vintage warbird pilot manual close by. Just like in my childhood, I am still reading and learning about these proud birds. I feel that I have been successful because I stuck to some very basic principles and some great guidance from my parents. I have also been blessed with unwavering support from my wife.

Here are some of my "Guides to Live By":
- Have a dream (goal)
- Make a plan for the accomplishment of that goal
- Make all short term activities relevant to the accomplishment of the long term goal
- Work hard for your goal
- Always keep the goal in mind, but be flexible on how that goal is achieved
- When presented with new temptations and distractions, remember the plan
- Life is full of choices
- Know yourself, believe in yourself
- Be responsible and accountable for your own happiness

I believe that these goals can be boiled down to a very simple tenet: find your passion; live your passion. It won't be easy. But it is worth the effort. You are worth the effort.

About the author:

Ed Finnegan holds an Airline Transport Pilot certificate with over 15,000 hours of flight time. He is a former U.S. Army aviator, now flying for a major airline.

As an airline pilot, Ed has flown the following aircraft: the Boeing 727, the Boeing 737, the Boeing 757, the Boeing 767, the Boeing 777, the Fokker F-100 and the McDonnell Douglas MD-80.

He is qualified on and flies several different warbirds ranging from WWII aircraft like the P-51 Mustang to the present day jet aircraft such as the Aero Vodochody AV-L39.

Ed resides in northern Illinois and may be reached at www.FinneganAviationServices.com.

FINDING PASSION AMIDST TRAGEDY

By Nancy Jo Nelson

"I am not what has happened to me. I am what I choose to become."

There are hidden gifts in tragedy. It stops time and marks a beginning of something new. It creates rawness and vulnerability to open the route to opportunities we never saw before. It rips away the facade and "going through the motion" ness of our mundane routine. You find out who in your life is strong enough to stay close so you can invest your time on those relationships. Life as you knew it is over and a blank book waits. So we have a choice: we can either write our own story or allow the event to write it for us. I choose to be the author and I am finding my passion daily.

"Life is not about waiting for the storm to pass. It's about learning to dance in the rain."

My tragedy brought my "fits and starts" life journey into fast track, turbo charged, laser focus. In a nutshell, when I finally grew strong enough to decide to end my marriage of 18 years, I had no idea my husband would disappear for five months before we found out he had ultimately ended his life. After I finally decided to finish my guilt trip, my children and I managed to wade through the chaos and pain of that time and finally arrive at a place of peace and new normalcy.

I decided early on that this event would not define me and would not cripple my children. It was messy, complicated and ugly at times. It was also humbling, revealing and sometimes even beautiful in a very poignant way. While I would never wish this event on my worst enemy, I would also not trade the exponential learning and growth we have experienced. It has been a HUGE transition for all of us and I realized early on that ALL transitions involve grief to some extent. Even the ones we choose. This life lesson has impacted my life beyond measure and has changed my very core. And it has led to me finding my passion for transition coaching.

All of us are going to face a tragedy, crisis or loss in this life. But here's the good news. If we can reframe these events as opportunities to be embraced and learned from rather to just endure and get through, we can normalize the experience as part of what makes us our amazing, complicated selves. We can become our authentic, passionate best. By staying present in the uncertainty of transition, we are more aware of the gifts. Allow me to share some observations I have made on my journey through the chaos. Take what works and leave the rest and may you find your passion wherever you are.

When tragedy smacks you in the face, you find out you are made of some pretty tough stuff and that you are capable of some pretty amazing things. You do things you never thought you could because you have to. You find out really quickly where to focus your limited energy and on whom. You stop wasting time and brain space on what other people think because the jig is up and your imperfect life is exposed. I found it incredibly freeing. However, this may make other people around you who are still caught up with what other people think very uncomfortable with your transparency. But that's ok. Let them worry if they want. Let them be uncomfortable. That is theirs. They own it. It isn't about you.

Stay in the present. If you need to, let yourself go to a worse case future scenario once in a while but ask yourself, "How likely is that to happen? Really?" Then bring yourself back to reality by breathing slowly and deeply. When we're stressed, we leave ourselves behind and go to places we don't belong yet. We end up holding our breath, starving ourselves of oxygen then hyperventilating, panicking. Stay in the present and breathe deeply! Sounds simple, but in times of stress and crisis, we forget. Breathing is a great way of bringing our focus back to the present.

Remember you ALWAYS have choices. You may feel very powerless over circumstances but you do have power. You can decide in each moment how to respond. And be okay with not responding at all because you're just plain tired and need a nap. Self-care is vitally important all the time but even more so when life feels upended.

Transitions and grief are a messy and imperfect science. We are all trailblazers in our journeys. I started asking myself the question, "Who said so?" as I found that most of my most stressful moments were a result of feeling like I "should" be doing something or doing it differently. When I asked myself that question, I found that usually my perceived failure was based on someone else's expectation, judgment or discomfort with the whole situation. When I could be aware enough to stop for a second and listen to my own heart and trust my intuition, I acted in a way that felt right and authentic to me. Peace would return. Remember there's a learning curve. Most of us have never done this life event before.

Personalize your grief process. Don't try to fit into anyone else's experience and stop gauging where you are in Kubler-Ross' stages of grief. Just be. Feel what you feel. Allow other people to grieve in their own way on their own timeframe too. My daughter's journey through her grief has been vastly different from my son's. Each person's connection to someone is uniquely theirs. By allowing them to find their own methods for coping and coming to terms with their new lives has allowed them to become resiliency heavyweights. They are both warriors in their own right. Let the advice from other people about how you should do this or that, where you should be by now, what they'd do in your situation, how they'd handle your children or life roll off with only their pure intention of trying to help sticking to you. Stop "shoulding" all over yourself.

You may have friends and even family move away from you emotionally. We humans like to solve problems and help people. When tragedy strikes, they can't fix it and often don't know how to help. So they distance themselves. Understandable. Yes. Comfortable. No. But wait! Here's the silver lining – there are people who have stuck by me and chosen to deal with their discomfort. I also have been amazed by the new relationships I have found either in spite of or because of my new path. Grieve the relationships and, for Pete's sake, try not to take it personally. Not everyone is cut out to be your walking buddy. Another gift of growth has been finding out that I am enough. On my own. I am learning to be my own best friend. Priceless.

And I implore you, allow yourself the time and space to grieve. My space finally came when I left my job two years after everything hit the fan. I had time to feel. To mourn everything that was. To contemplate and journal and reflect. That's where I had the most growth. I needed that downtime to grow and stretch myself. To debunk much of what I thought I knew and to discover how this horrendous tragedy could turn into an unexpected route to my passion. And I crossed a bucket list item off by finally finishing my degree.

Be gentle with yourself. This grief thing is tricky. Even when you think you have done everything to prepare for that holiday season, anniversary, birthday, grief can blindside you in a moment that you least expect. I have found that the anticipation of these significant days is far more difficult than the actual day itself. My advice for fellow grievers is to just ride the wave as it comes and hold on to the knowledge that the wave eventually takes you to shore. You'll get through it and you will do it. Time really does heal. It has a way of softening the hard edges of grief and creating something new and brilliant in its place. Like beach glass.

Work on forgiveness. Forgive yourself. Forgive the circumstance. Forgive the relationship. Forgive the universe. Forgive. It's hard but necessary work and is the way to keeping you from getting hard and bitter. It's a process. Trust it.

I cannot stress this enough: TAKE CARE OF YOU! Those flight attendants know what they're talking about when they tell you to put on your oxygen mask first before helping those around you. If you don't take care of yourself, you cannot take care of anyone else. This was a hard lesson for me and ran counter to all the "shoulds" in my life surrounding motherhood. But it is true. With a capital T.

I believe we are created for relationships. If we fully invest in them, there will be pain in the transitions of life. We are hardwired to grieve as a normal process of being human. It's only when we struggle to suck it up and move on that it cripples us because an emotion denied comes out through the side. So grieve in your way, in your time. To stuff or deny it cheapens the impact of that relationship in our lives. It does a disservice to the one gone and to you. Remember, you are the boss of your grief. It belongs to you. Trust yourself. You will be amazed. When the fog clears, you just might find your passion. It was waiting for you to discover all along. Maybe, just maybe, tragedy brings us back to the basics of who we really are.

> "Promise me you'll always remember: You're braver than you believe, and stronger than you seem, and smarter than you think." A. A. Milne.

About the author:

Combine a ton of real life experience, a wicked sense of humor, resiliency and fearlessness, pack it all in five feisty feet and what do you get? A transition and grief coach named **Nancy Jo Nelson** who will help you move forward and unleash your own "Warrior Within". We have more in common than you think. For another taste, visit www.warriorwithincoaching.com.

Tails of My Life

By Dale Nelson

PASSION...The word alone invokes images of love, intensity, even sensuality. What is passion to me? It is the one thing that I feel so strongly about that my voice raises two octaves when I am talking and I tear up just thinking about it.

What is my passion? The one and only thing that can do all of those things to me...animal rescue.

Unbeknownst to me, I did my first rescue at age five. I was playing at the park down the street from where I lived (something that you could do fifty years ago) when I heard a soft crying sound coming from a garbage can. Inside was a newborn kitten, no more than two days old. I ran home to get my mom and after talking to the vet who felt it would not live, we took a chance and fed it every two hours with a doll bottle. That newborn kitten that was not supposed to live made it to sixteen years old. Hence, my love (obsession) with animals began. Over the years, countless homeless cats were smuggled into the house, as my dad did not share the same love of animals as my mom and I did.

In my youth there was not a heart that I did not want to heal, a homeless person I did not want to feed, or an animal that I did not want to take home. I realized early on that I could not save the world, so I chose a corner of that world that I could make a difference in, one where there was no voice speaking for them. I felt that if everyone could just take a corner to work on, maybe, just maybe, we could meet in the middle.

Over the years my love for animals focused on basset hounds. I fell in love with their long silky ears and sad droopy eyes. After buying my first basset from a pet store eighteen years ago, one of my patients at my dental office told me I should talk to her mother whom did Basset rescue. Basset rescue? What is Basset rescue? I had no clue there was a rescue group for Basset Hounds, let alone for every dog and cat breed imaginable. Not to mention, rescue groups that do all breeds of cats and dogs.

Years later, and countless homeless animals that I have helped rescue and re-home, I have found my purpose in life. My specialty is rehabilitating abused dogs. I strongly feel love and patience cures all. By the time they leave my house they know there will be food in their tummies, that a hand will not hit them, a foot will not kick them and above all, that they are loved. My three children used to "tease" me that I loved the dogs more than I loved them. I told them, "When I was five, I didn't want you, I wanted them." Fortunately, I did not scar them for life, they are all huge animal lovers too, just not Basset Hounds.

One of the most rewarding experiences I have ever had was rescuing animals after Hurricane Katrina. A plea went out looking for foster homes for the dogs displaced during the hurricane. I got a call early one morning letting me know I had a Coonhound coming in a few days. Turned out her owner had drowned and her time at the pound was running out. Thanks to social media I was able to find her a great home.

The next dog we got was another Coonhound. I named her Katie, after Katrina. She had recently had puppies, was emaciated and suffering from heartworm. The government was paying for her heartworm treatment and she was almost thru with it when she suddenly bloated in the middle of the night. We rushed her to the emergency vet where I was told I had five minutes to make a decision as to whether or not to do surgery, as she would be dead in an hour. The cost of the surgery was at least $5,500. I looked at my husband and asked, "What do we do?"

He said, "You do what you have to do to walk out of this door. If you can't put her down, we do the surgery."

At the time, we had two children in college, but I felt so strongly that she did not survive the hurricane, stayed alive by eating garbage and make it all the way to me to die. I was so convinced she would survive the surgery that I told the surgeon to go ahead and save her life. The surgery was a success and he said if they could keep her alive twenty-four hours she would make it. At twenty three hours she threw an embolism and died.

My passion died along with Katie. I told my husband I could not do this anymore. My heart just could not break in any more pieces. Plus, we now owed $7,300 and had no dog. Fast forward six weeks...my rescue partner called me from the pound in Mississippi and she was crying. In the same stall where Katie had been, there was a nine month old Coonhound, just like Katie. He was lying there shivering and terrified. A local hunter had let all of his Coonhounds go after the hurricane, as there was nothing left to hunt, and animal control picked this little guy up, hovering in a ditch. The people at the pound knew how devastated I was after losing Katie, so they offered to send him to me; otherwise they were gassing him the next day. Once more I turned to my husband and asked, "What do we do?"

He replied, "Bring him home." When Andy came home to me, he brought my passion back with him.

For the next two years, our four person rescue group was able to re-home over 1,100 dogs and cats from Mississippi. I spent ten days down there in the pound pulling over one hundred dogs and cats for that transport. Unfortunately, for everyone we saved, there were thousands that were gassed due to overcrowding in the pounds. I, however, learned a valuable lesson from my time in Mississippi; not to sweat the small stuff. A week after I got back, Andy, my Katrina dog, broke a table that held all my crystal. As I was sweeping up hundreds of dollars worth of vases and bowls, my friend commented on how calm I was. My response was, "I have just spent ten days in Mississippi with people who are living in FEMA trailers who have nothing but the clothes on their backs and hope in their hearts. Am I really going to worry about some broken crystal?"

The people in Mississippi were not the only ones who have changed my outlook on life. I have learned quite a bit from my four legged creatures.

The Top Ten Lessons I Learned From My Rescue Dogs

10) When a dog gets skunked, we think it smells like sulfuric acid. They think it smells like Chanel #5.

9) Douche is the only thing that will remove the above mentioned skunk smell.

8) A Great Dane thinks it is a Chihuahua.

7) A Chihuahua thinks it is a Great Dane.

6) Your bra makes a great tug of war toy.

5) Your new shoes make an even greater chew toy.

4) Toilet paper was meant to be spread around the backyard.

3) If it is food they will eat it, unless it is lima beans. No one likes lima beans.

2) If you don't put it away, it is fair game. My bad!

1) They will greet you with the same love in their eyes even if you have just gone outside and come back in. Always.

In the last eighteen years I have had sixty foster dogs and eleven "forever fosters" or "foster failures," as we in the rescue world call it. I have lost countless shoes, socks, blankets, too many articles of clothes to mention, as well as a bathroom floor (don't even ask)! However, the love, the laughter, the slobber, that I received in return far outweighs the losses. There is nothing like waking up on a Sunday morning, cuddling with seven hound dogs, one of them being a 170 pound bloodhound, to start the day off with a smile.

My dream in life is to open a sanctuary, so when someone dumps their seventeen year old blind and deaf dog at the pound, they will have somewhere safe to live out the rest of their lives in a home environment. I want a place for "unadoptables" as well as those looking for their "fur"ever homes to have a place to run and a bed to sleep in. There would be a twenty-four hour affordable vet hospital, so if your dog bloats in the middle of the night, you won't have to decide their fate based on the cost factor. My goal is to make adopting and owning a pet affordable for their lifetime.

My other goal is to educate people about the plight of the homeless animal. There are anywhere from four to eight million dogs and cats euthanized every year. Every eight seconds an animal is put down. We advocate, "Please adopt, don't shop." If you cannot adopt, foster. If you cannot foster, volunteer, donate and help spread the word. If rescue groups do not have foster homes, they cannot pull an animal from a kill pound and save its life. Spay and neuter your pets, microchip them, keep them safe, and above all, love and protect them. They are for life, theirs, not yours.

Every time a foster leaves, they take a piece of my heart, but what they leave behind is a lifetime of memories. I may have saved their lives, but in retrospect, they have saved mine. They were what I was missing in my life and in my heart to make me complete.

> You came to me broken and bruised
>
> Never again will you be abused
>
> I fed you, I loved you, I gave you a home
>
> You will never again be alone
>
> I made you strong-gave you wings to fly
>
> When you leave I won't let you see me cry
>
> You are now healed, you are now whole
>
> You will forever be my heart and soul

My boss said to me recently "You are so going to Heaven."

I replied, "I don't want to go to Heaven, I want to go to the Rainbow Bridge where all my babies are."

His response was, "That is just a subdivision of Heaven." You know what? I kinda like that.

About the author:

Aside from volunteering in the animal rescue world for the last eighteen years, **Dale Nelson** has been in the dental field for almost forty years. She is happily married for twenty-eight years to my hubby Mark, who supports my passion in life, with a lot of eye rollings and "yes, dear"s. Along with her seven "forever fosters" she has three furless children. Samantha, a licensed clinical psychologist, Jennifer, a licensed cosmetologist, and Brett, a police officer. She has two sons in laws, Kirk, a high school band director and Matt, a State Trooper.

You can find Dale on Facebook, Dale Trackman Nelson www.facebook.com/dale.trackmannelson, as well as her two main rescue groups:

A Heart For Animals www.aheartforanimals.org/

Rescue Warriors Corp www.shelterexchange.org/

Your Passion Can Adapt To Change, Just As You Do

By Terry League

Sometimes the journey to discovering and igniting your passion is more of an awakening, or the realization of a desire that was always there.

Passion is a reason to get up every morning; it is what motivates you to be your best. For me, igniting my passion means that I am in tune with my talents, while finding the best way to use those talents to help others.

My story focuses on how to first recognize your true passion, and then let it evolve as the events in your life change. With a little patience and flexibility, I learned that there is more than one way to use your passion to make a difference.

When I was younger, I wanted to be a teacher. I played "school" with my dolls and tried to teach – or boss around – my younger brother. I could picture myself as a schoolteacher someday and that idea stayed with me through my early years.

However, as I finished high school and prepared for college, I no longer had an interest in teaching school. I did not really know what career path to choose. So I decided to major in business, because it seemed like a safe, practical option when nothing else appealed to me. It was a broad field and even though I did not know what I was going to do with my business degree, I figured I would narrow it down to finance, management, or marketing by the time I graduated. Fortunately, I chose to concentrate in marketing, because that proved to be a necessary skill in almost all the jobs I held since then.

My required business classes usually were not all that fun for me, so I took as many history classes as I could fit in my schedule. Yes, a history class was fun!

History had not always been my favorite subject, but once I got to college and took a few history classes as electives, I really enjoyed them! Some of my favorite history classes were Ancient Egyptian history, European/Great Britain studies and Historical Archaeology. Studying past civilizations, as well as ancient cultures and customs were fascinating topics to me. I still enjoy learning and reading about history and cultures.

Before I realized it, I had enough credits to declare a minor in history. It was around that time that I started to entertain the idea of teaching history after I graduated, instead of going into what I considered the more mundane field of business.

I always enjoyed studying something, organizing the related information and presenting it in a way that helped others learn it too. I realized that I wanted to teach more than I wanted to work in the business world, and at the time, I thought those two were completely separate options.

I felt like I had discovered my true passion! I was going to teach others about a subject I loved – ancient history. At the time, this new career path required a Master's degree, so I started graduate work the semester immediately after completing my undergraduate business degree.

In addition to taking graduate classes, I was working full-time at a large company that hired me right after graduation. It was an entry-level position and a low-stress job that would allow me plenty of time to concentrate on my graduate work.

At the same time, I was also planning and organizing my wedding. My soon-to-be husband, David, and I were getting married in October. He had graduated from the same college and was working in his first job as well.

But my graduate work only lasted one semester. I was stressed, tired of exams and became disillusioned with my dream of teaching history. Looking back now, after raising three children, it is somewhat hard to believe that I could not handle the stress of a job, a part-time school schedule and a wedding. That "stress" was minor compared to the later stress I experienced when juggling motherhood and a business!

I realized that the teaching career I wanted to pursue would require a doctorate degree, which meant more years in graduate school than I had originally planned. Since we were on a limited budget, I would have had to continue working full-time so I could attend school on a part-time basis. I figured my current stressful situation would continue for a quite a few more years and I quickly lost my desire to spend all that time in school. So I set those plans aside and left graduate school.

However, that decision was for the best, because within six months, the company that I worked for decided to start an internal training program. This program would train employees from branches all over the country on how to use the custom-built software in our sales support department. My boss offered me the chance to develop this program from the ground floor up. I would be creating the training program and materials, writing a reference manual for the trainees and conducting each training session. I loved it!

I had found my teaching passion again! I enjoyed everything about my new job. From planning the training modules to writing all the required materials, it was very rewarding to put a complete program together and call it my own. Working with my students was even more rewarding. Trainees would come from their branch to my location for two weeks of intensive training. Each student's needs were different, and the flexible nature of the training program allowed me to customize the pace and modules for each person.

I realized from this experience that my true passion was simply teaching; it did not necessarily matter what subject matter I was sharing. I enjoyed the process of putting a program together and watching my students learn. For many of my trainees, this was one of their first experiences either with the company, as many were new hires, or with this type of software program. They left with a good understanding of their new job, along with a mastery of some new computer skills and I felt great about the job I was doing.

After a few years in the corporate world, I made the decision to leave my job to stay home full-time when my first daughter was born. Fast forward five years and I was now home full-time with three daughters. My passion for teaching took another turn with motherhood.

Every day holds a teachable moment as a parent and I enjoyed the time spent with my girls. I gave up a training position in the corporate world, but over the years found other ways to pursue my passion for teaching others. In addition to those teachable parenting moments, I took on leadership roles as a volunteer in various community groups, taught Sunday school for several years and even worked as a teacher's aide at my kids' school.

I was also part of several home-based, direct sales companies over the years. While I enjoyed working with those companies, I was definitely not a very strong salesperson. For me, the best part of the experience was teaching others how to work from home and balance a family with a career.

When my husband decided to start his own computer consulting business, we both became brand new "students". We had to learn how to set up, market and run a business from square one. My degree in business/marketing came in handy as I focused solely on helping him launch and run the business.

My administrative duties in our computer business did not offer many teaching opportunities, but what I learned during that time now helps me teach other business owners how to juggle social media marketing and day-to-day business operations.

Once social media took the world by storm, I saw an opportunity to use both areas of my expertise, marketing and training, to further pursue my teaching passion. I now enjoy developing training programs that help other business owners use social media in their marketing efforts.

So in a way, I have come full circle from my college days, when I first realized that teaching was my passion and desired career path. I may not have ended up teaching the subject matter or the students I originally imagined – no one could have told me then that I would be a social media trainer twenty years down the road. But my story is an example of how it is important to first recognize your passion and then remain flexible in the ways that you put it to good use.

We sometimes hold ourselves back by focusing on an ideal image of how to use our passion. For me, the ideal image of teaching others was working at a college. When I left graduate school, I thought my chance to teach was over. However, you never know what opportunities may appear down the road or how a major change in the world will create a brand-new path for your passion. If someone had told me twenty years ago that I would someday be helping global clients who I met online through social media while sitting at my desk in Florida, I never would have believed them!

The point is to stay committed to your passion while being open to new ways of sharing it. It may grow and develop into something very different from what you first imagined, as I felt my passion for teaching did over the years.

Another important point is to stay in tune with whom you really are, no matter what changes take place around you. At each point on my career path, I did not realize at the time how my passion for teaching others was guiding my decisions. I continued to wonder what my ideal career would be, only to realize later that each job along the way was centered on teaching and those jobs were leading me to the point I am at today.

So how do you find your passion if you do not have one now?

Start by being honest with yourself; it is not your family or friend's life-story you are creating. It is yours! Think of the things that others compliment you on and ask yourself if there is a common theme.

For example, do the people around you always ask, "How do you do that?" or, "How are you so good at that?" For me, the question was always, "How can you be so organized with three kids?"

Believe me when I say that my house, the laundry and the kitchen were never shining examples of organization. It was the systems, the schedules, and the family management that I could organize well. Those same skills relate directly to my teaching or training programs today: the detailed organization of ideas or systematic processes.

Consider the following questions: What do you enjoy doing now? What have you enjoyed doing in the past? The answers may help you determine an underlying passion.

Is there something you are always helping friends and family with? This is exactly how my husband started the computer business. Friends and family were always calling him with computer problems. He was their go-to source for all things computer-related and now he is the go-to source for small and mid-size businesses that have become clients.

Learn something new. With the Internet, we have immediate access to so many more things today than when I started my career search over twenty years ago. You may find a new passion or a new way to tune into an existing passion.

Volunteer in your community, take a class and discover something new in your own backyard. There may be a need you can fill right now with your talents. Maybe that will turn into a passion. On the other hand, it might be a stepping-stone that leads to the discovery of a new passion.

When my daughters took ballet classes, I was a very active volunteer at their dance studios. Being a part of the ballet world again was amazing in itself, because as a child, I lasted a total of five days as a ballerina when my mother enrolled me in classes. The music my teacher played from Peter and the Wolf scared me and I came home crying every day.

Thankfully, my daughters did not get their dancing skills from me, but I put my organizational skills to good use as a volunteer. I helped backstage with costume changes and the organization of volunteer schedules, as well as with the marketing of special events. I also volunteered my time to create a website for one of the studios in the early days of website development. This project helped me learn more about websites and online marketing, which later became a service I offered my clients and taught others how to do.

As time goes on and you grow, your passion may grow with you in ways you never expected. I am a big believer in the idea that you should never stop learning and whether it is personal growth or career-oriented growth, those new skills can only help your passion in the long run.

If you believe that you already know what your passion is, I encourage you to look a little deeper at the ways in which you can develop it. What are your strengths and weaknesses? What do you need to do to turn a weakness into a strength? Do you need more education, a mentor or a coach? It is important for me to continue my training because the world of social media is always changing, but no matter what the industry or cause you believe in, there is always something new to learn.

Do you keep up with local and global trends? Do you think there may be a way for you to use your passion in three years or five years down the road? Do not get stuck in the "now" or the day-to-day challenges of your immediate situation.

I did not understand how performing the somewhat dull, administrative tasks for our computer business could help me pursue my teaching passion, but the skills required for setting up daily systems and processes are applicable to developing training programs for my clients. I needed that experience in organization and project management back then to prepare me for the work I do today.

Be your own biggest cheerleader, not your own worst critic! You will have doubts, mistakes and failures along the way to discovering your passion. But do not stop. Look at each challenge as a learning experience. Every mistake or obstacle can also contain a lesson and in the end, most successful people will tell you that they would not be where they are today without their mistakes.

Finding your passion and putting it into action does not necessarily happen overnight. You may be developing your passion, and discovering new ways to use it, for many years to come. Your whole lifetime may be the journey and that is okay too.

No one says you have to find your passion when you are young. It may take years before you discover your passion or before you realize that it's been there all along, quietly waiting for the right opportunity to come along.

It is never too late to ignite your passion! As George Eliot so wisely said, "It is never too late to be what you might have been."

About the author:

Terry League is Co-Founder, Social Media Consultant at League Computer Solutions, Inc., and a founding member of the Global Social Media Managers Association.

She holds a B.S. degree in Marketing with a minor in History, and has experience in corporate training. As a small business owner herself, Terry knows the social media challenges small businesses face.

Contact Terry for information on social media training programs, coaching, and account management.

Email: terry@leaguecomputers.com
Website: www.leaguecomputers.com
Twitter: www.twitter.com/terryleague

Style Your Home, Style Your Life

By Kristine Porter

"What one loves in childhood stays in the heart forever."

This quote by Mary Jo Putney gives a glimpse of the source of my passion for redesigning rooms. Growing up as the youngest of five children, I had to make do with what was handed down to me. Fortunately, I found it fun to refashion my furniture to make it my style.

Today I am delighted to help others re-style their rooms, giving a custom designed look without buying new things. How is that possible? By listening to the story of the person who lives there, asking questions, digging deeper, and then reusing things in a fresh new way.

There is a five step process to redesigning a room and it works well for redesigning a busy schedule too. Each step must be complete before moving on…not just thinking about doing it, but truly doing the hard work of finishing the step. This process delivers amazing results; things you'd never imagine before beginning.

The Five Step Redesign Process

Step 1: Clear the room. Take everything out starting with the smallest items, removing things hanging on the walls and remove the big furniture as well. Be sure to put like pieces together in another room.

Step 1: Figuratively -- If you're doing this figuratively, whilst redesigning your schedule, you'll write a list of everything you do in a given month – being sure to put like things together. You'll want to see your entire schedule with all of the little things and bigger things "removed" so you can reevaluate them. It might be time to refresh and repurpose those things that no longer serve you well.

Step 2: Evaluate the room's purpose. You determine the function of this space (not the previous owner). Do you need a cozy study more than a never used dining room? Be careful not to have more than three functions dedicated to one room, or it will begin to feel chaotic. For example a bedroom/exercise/office/craft/storage room will be a space you won't want to ever go in.

Step 2: Figuratively – you determine the schedule for you best life. What makes the best use of your gifts, talents, interests and time? Be careful about running in too many different directions because that produces chaos in life.

Step 3: Place the biggest furniture first. Face the focal point(s) with the biggest furniture, then group them into a conversational setting. Make sure your seated furniture is cohesive in the grouping yet has enough personal space to feel comfortable when people are seated. There may be cultural differences with personal space allowances too. There are several different ways to accomplish this depending on room shape, furniture size and purpose.

Step 3: Figuratively – put the most important things in your life first, but make sure all things are connected with appropriate space and rest.

Step 4: Add light and life. Every room should have at least three lamps to be warm and inviting. Each room needs its own life-personality to tell the story of the people who live there. Ever wonder why you feel so drawn to certain spaces? It's because of the room's story resonates with us. Hang artwork and/or photos that depict the passions of the owners.

Step 4: Figuratively – add those little things into your schedule that "light you up" and excite you. Your days can be abundant when you work in your strengths and do the things that bring you joy. Minimize your weaknesses, which are not necessarily things you don't do well, but by definition are things that weaken or exhaust you to do. Is there someone else who is delighted to do those same things? Find her. Get it off your list.

Step 5: Accessorize – this is like putting on the room's jewelry. You know that old saying about the key to the right look - get dressed up and put on all your jewelry, then take one piece off to know you have the right amount. Accessories in a room are like that too. You need a place for the eye to rest and a place to wander, so don't over-do-it with accessories. You want to place things in odd numbers because your eye will divide even numbers and look at the space in between.

Step 5 Figuratively – adding the "jewelry of life" is putting those things in your schedule that make you sparkle... that are a joy for you. Be careful not to overdo this step; take just one thing off your list before you complete your schedule.

I use this five step process when I want to redesign a change in my life. It is much easier for me to change a room in someone else's home because I am not as emotionally attached to the items. I listen to the homeowner, and ask probing questions to find out what they truly love. Only after learning about their story, will I take on the work of the re-styling a room...and the results have been amazing.

One of my clients was a woman whose father was terminally ill. She had just returned from visiting him and brought home several mementos from his life. She had a pile of things left on her kitchen table for us to incorporate into her family room, along with a new family photo for the room. She was overwhelmed with a mixture of emotions and a pile of "What should I do with this?" items.

She left the home, and we got to work, beginning with the emptying the room. We followed all five steps:
- Emptied the room
- Evaluated the purpose as a place to come together as a family.
- Placed the sofa, love seat and two chairs in a circle-of-conversation for more people to sit and relax.
- Added four lamps to the room, to be warm and inviting and hung the family photo over the fireplace. We also hung some shelves to display a few antique bottles and tins.

• Accessorizing the room always takes the most time, but brings the best results. We grouped a few collectibles on the mantle and placed a plant on the other side to give life and softness. As your eye traveled around the room, the look was unified and told the story of happy family memories.

When the homeowner returned three hours later to see her finished family room, the tears of joy flowed. She said, "I am losing my father to this world and feel like he's still with me in my home. The beauty of his life is here. I love the way you have chosen a few meaningful pieces to tell our story. I was too overwhelmed to decide what to use and what to pack away. Now I can relax and enjoy my FAMILY room."

This is why I love styling homes and teaching others to do this too. Sometimes people just need a little help to make final decisions on accessories, and other times rooms just aren't working the way the builder determined.

Another client loved to entertain her big family and many friends with dinner parties. Her house had a tiny dining room, but a large living room that went unused. We applied the five step process to both rooms, giving her a new small library/study room and a large dining room for entertaining with food, friends and fun. Before re-styling, she was looking at plans to knock the wall out in her dining room and remove a half bath so she could have more space. After the restyle, she uses both rooms so much more, and her husband was happy to NOT have the reconstruction costs.

My challenge for you is to just start with one room or one month in your schedule and apply all five steps in order. You will be amazed at the difference you can make.

About the author:

If you are interested in pursuing your home styling passion as a profitable income stream, contact **Kristine Porter** at www.StylingAndStaging.com for information on the Professional Certification program to become a Home Stylist and House Stager.

In an intensive program, you can learn via hands-on training, along with classroom work, to have your own business following your passion for home decorating.

SAY YES, WITH ENTHUSIASM

By Michaline Sowatzke

Toastmasters is a non-profit organization that meets in individual clubs to promote better listening, thinking and speaking. When I first joined twenty-five years ago it was because I was passed over for a promotion I thought I deserved. My focus was on improving my speaking skills and presenting a more professional image.

Within the first year of joining Toastmasters my life was shattered. I got divorced, my Illinois office of eight hundred Eastern Airlines employees was closing and I chose to stay with the company and transfer to North Carolina. Within a month of moving to Charlotte, my twenty-eight year old brother died from aneurism in his brain. Here I was 800 miles from home without friends and family. That is when I read in the Toastmasters magazine that the Regional Conference was being held in town. I walked up to the registration table and the gentleman said, "What club do you belong to?" I explained that I was new in town, and was still shopping for a club.

He walked out from behind the table gave me a big bear hug and said, "You're with us!"

Just the fact that I was a member of Toastmasters opened doors for me. I was asked to join the team presenting the United Way Campaign at my company. We went to a rally, had a team of presenters and all went well on the day shift. Then I suddenly found myself covering the midnight shift workers all by myself. There I was handing out the pledge cards, showing a film, then giving a presentation, collecting the pledge cards and setting it all up again for the next group. Without my Toastmasters training, I never would have had the confidence to do this all by myself.

Still very new in the program I met my mentor, Richard Hamilton, he looked exactly like Barney Fife, and even carried the one bullet in his pocket. He said, "Whenever someone from Toastmasters asks you to do something, say "Yes" with enthusiasm." A little over a year after I moved to Charlotte, Eastern Airlines closed its doors for good. My very first nephew was born in Chicago and I had a precious little reason to be back at home with a new career as a travel agent.

Then the phone call came, it was Mike Burnham the Toastmasters District Governor, asking me to chair the spring conference. Wait a minute, I've been in Toastmasters less than two years, I had been away from Chicago for the last year and a half, I really don't know a soul, but I heard those haunting words, "Say yes with enthusiasm," so I said yes. I had twelve years experience in Girl Scouts and had attended various conferences, so I started assembling THE TEAM.

From that bear hug beginning so very many years ago, I have had the good fortune of visiting over 100 different Toastmasters clubs in such far away places as Japan and South Africa. They all share the same hospitality and enthusiasm and profess our motto:

"We provide a supportive and positive learning experience in which members are empowered to develop communication and leadership skills, resulting in greater self-confidence and personal growth."

This is the value of participating with gusto.

About the author:

Michaline Sowatzke's heart and soul is in the fast paced and ever changing world of corporate travel. A client once said that she has a servant's heart, loves what she does and it shows. With 35 years in the business, she had a variety of experiences starting with Eastern Airlines, on site at law firms and now with FROSCH specializes in luxury travel.

Her loving Chicago family, twelve years in Girl Scouts and distinguished service as the District Governor in Toastmasters, has shaped her into the person that she is today. Michaline is active in her church, Sts. Peter and Paul, in Cary, Illinois. Contact her at toastmastersfoxvalley@yahoo.com.

DETERMINATION: FRIEND OR FOE?

By Dorothy Robin

PART 1 - SINK OR SWIM

Jeff had a problem. (Truthfully, Jeff is not his real name - it has been mercifully changed to protect the fine, innocent young man.) Jeff's problem was that he wanted to be IN the water and OUT of the water - both at the same time. In truth, he wanted to be able to jump into deep water (actually, he really wanted to stay out of the water at all costs), but his goal was to jump into the deep end and then swim four continuous lengths of the pool. That's it. Pretty simple for someone who is comfortable with the water and can swim. Pretty earth shatteringly impossible for someone who has had a debilitating experience in the water and will avoid trying to learn to swim at all costs.

Jeff had a marvelous opportunity: while at a summer camp he had the opportunity to learn to swim. An opportunity that he signed up for…and then spent the entire lesson time in the shower room in order to avoid getting into the pool. Totally understandable to me. After all, as a teenager my father almost drowned - twice - and that made him insistent that all his kids would take swimming lessons and learn to swim. (Yeah for Dad & Mom!) Of course, I wasn't cheering either of my parents during my first few lessons…instead, I was standing in the little pool shivering with fear while my teacher and the rest of the kids easily submerged their heads (ALL the way under the water) to have a "tea party" on the bottom of the pool. I felt left out; I felt scared; I wanted to go home.

Ah, but life isn't always about feelings, is it? Sometimes it's about what one needs to do (either self-imposed, or parentally-imposed by those loving people who gave birth to us and want the best for us even though we're scared to death).

Long story short: I learned to swim, learned to love the water, became a Red Cross certified Swim Instructor and happily began teaching children how to swim. Helping people - I loved it! Seeing their progress - so exciting! Working with scared swimmers to help them overcome their fear - makes me grin from ear to ear the rest of the day.

My dad was even inspired to take swimming lessons; not with me at first. He sadly he had a bad experience with a swim teacher who laughed at him. Note: don't make fun of someone because they're scared - know that everyone is scared of something so work with them to the best of your ability to help them overcome their fear. Later Dad asked me to work with him. I'm so proud of him: petrified and highly wanting to avoid the water, he was determined to learn to swim enough to save himself if he fell into water. He did learn to swim and voluntarily went to the pool on several occasions without me just to practice. I am so very proud of him.

So when Jeff and I met, and Jeff wanted to overcome his fear of water to learn to swim - I empathized with him. Jeff and I met at the YMCA's pool and our work together began. Literally every five minutes he'd need to get out of the water to go use the bathroom. (You know what it's like being anxious or apprehensive about something - it makes you need to...you know...use the bathroom.) Jeff said it was due to the water seeping into his skin through his pores - I didn't correct him. We kept working together and because of his incredible determination, he learned enough to float by himself, then to do a simple stroke, then to make it half way across the pool.

On and on, week after week, this highly intelligent, tenacious young man kept coming back and was able to progress more and more. It came to the point where Jeff was only leaving the pool every 10 minutes to use the bathroom. Finally, his personal due-date was fast approaching. I told him there was no pressure - I'd come back to meet with him as many times as it took. I told him to just relax and remember that he had done various lengths of the pool before, and he had the strength and ability to do the four lengths in a row. He jumped in the deep end (I was constantly in the water with him - every stroke of the way) and he headed determinedly toward the shallow end. Upon reaching the end he wanted to stop, but I lovingly hollered at him to keep going!

As he was swimming, I reminded him to slow down and take his time, to breathe and let the water hold him up. He swam to the deep end again, turned around and headed for the shallow end... the fourth length...the end in sight. When Jeff reached the end the entire pool rang with my shouts of joy: "You did it! Great job! You DID it! Fantastic work!" The beam on his face could have lit up an entire lighthouse. What a determined young man - I am so proud of him.

PART 2 - TO BE DETERMINED OR NOT - THAT IS THE QUESTION…

Determination. Great word, isn't it? Great especially when I'm working with determined people to try and help them. Not so great when I have to actually be determined myself - that actually takes work. Now, don't get me wrong - I indeed frequently shirked hard work when I was younger. But as I got older (ok, I really didn't get older - I actually had the marvelous experience of staying 27 years old for many years in a row. Pretty do-able until around 40 and then I had to admit that I've actually had a few birthdays of a number higher than 27…) as I lived life longer, the work ethic kicked in. I was determined to do my best in every area of life, willing to work for it, wanting to learn and grow as a person.

But, did you know that determination can actually be counter-productive on occasion? (You may be determined to ignore that comment, but, sometimes being too determined can indeed be counter-productive as you will see in the following story.)

About fourteen years ago I was carrying my young toddler downstairs, misstepped, slipped, fell, and dislocated my shoulder. Thank God the baby was perfectly fine. I had my older daughter care for him while I lay for a frightening time, immobile on the floor, not knowing what to do. Long story short, in the process of carefully getting up, my shoulder slipped back into place.

Two weeks later, my little toddler was acting up in the back seat of the car, so I reached back to take the toy from him. Big mistake. Big, huge mistake. Shoulder slipped out of the socket again. I managed to single-handedly maneuver the car into the nearest driveway and stop the car. There was a business sign, with a business phone number on that sign and I made what is probably the strangest phone call they ever received: "Excuse me, but does anyone there know how to put a dislocated shoulder back into place? I'm in your driveway right now." They responded wisely by calling an ambulance. In the process of getting out the car, my shoulder slipped into place again. After that, the doctor prescribed physical therapy to strengthen the shoulder. I was determined to never have it slip out again.

Fast forward 10 years. I had determinedly poured myself into my kids, my family, and my work - and equally as determined - ignored my own health. Time to get in shape again! No problem, I thought: I am a swimmer - I can easily lose weight and get back into shape.

There I was in the Lake Geneva YMCA pool: a former lifeguard and swimming instructor, in the shallow end of the lap pool, out of breath, heart racing and arm numb...after only a few laps. Have you ever had a strong sense of identity (you know who you are! You are the person who can fix anything, you are the basketball player, you are the top reader in the summer library reading program...) Have you ever had a strong sense of identity, and then had it suddenly snatched away from you? I had my identity stolen away from me and it took a lot of baby steps to try to get it back.

I was scared of the water, but my parents MADE each of us kids take swimming lessons at the YMCA so we would know how to swim. Baby step by baby step, I learned how to love the water, became a lifeguard and a swimming instructor. Who was I? I was a lifeguard and swimming instructor at the YMCA during high school and college. Other than that, I was scared, shy and didn't know who I was.

Fast forward: married, later had three wonderful children. It was mandatory to me that I taught each of them to swim. After all, my dad almost drowned twice, which was why he made us learn to swim.

A few years ago, my son crossed over into Boy Scouts and that opened up a new world of growth opportunities for me. When I learned that the scouts could earn a one mile swim patch, I encouraged them to work on that, but then thought, "Wait a minute! Now I need to do it, too, to set a good example." I always tell my kids I won't ask them to do anything that I am not willing to do. Hey, no problem! I swam for fun in high school and college, and I can baby step up to a mile.

So, I got my swim suit, went to the YMCA, got in the water and swam down a length and back. Again, swam down and back. That was it! My heart was racing (boy, was I out of shape apparently) and worse...my arm felt numb. This was going to take a lot of humbling baby steps for me to get up to even a quarter mile! I left the pool that day, but was determined to reach that mile. I kept coming back, kept working on improving little by little, and after many months was able to get to 72 lengths - one mile! Wah-HOO! Who am I? I am a swimmer!

In the meantime, at scouts I joined the committee, took over the newsletter, was the Activities Coordinator, went camping with the scouts when another adult was needed and became a Merit Badge Counselor. Not only was I a Swimming Merit Badge Counselor but a Personal Fitness Counselor. "Ok, I thought, I'm overweight and still out of shape. I can't promote personal fitness to the boys if I'm not in shape." Back to the pool I went. By baby steps, I built up to going two times a week, swimming one mile each time: front crawl down, breast stroke back - 72 lengths. "I'm a swimmer!!"

And then it happened. My shoulder had been feeling stiff for years due to the dislocation - I just ignored it and went on with life: digging holes to plant trees, playing catch with my kids, gardening...you name it, I could do it.

Two years ago, I decided to go to the physical therapist to 'fix' the tightness in my shoulder. I told him what the problem was, that I was swimming one mile two times each week. During the process the shoulder improved. I wish I stopped there. Instead, I kept going and the physical therapist kept increasing the weights and the exercises every time I came. All of a sudden, during a swim after PT, my arm started hurting badly - so I stopped.

In hindsight, I now know that my arm had been overworked and I had my first tendinitis. Instead of healing, I was no longer able to do all those fun things, because each little stress on the arm brought back the tendinitis. I couldn't swim, couldn't dig holes in the ground and couldn't throw a ball with my children. Nothing. In a way, I lost my identity. Finally, after a grueling experience physically, financially and emotionally, the long term pain began the process of going away and I was able to wipe the kitchen counter without too much pain.

Swimming? Not yet, but I was determined to get back there. After a summer of determinedly doing nothing (that would fix it, right?) I had done a magnificent job of atrophying my muscles in both arms, and finally agreed to go to a different physical therapist to regain strength. I was determined, and got slowly stronger, but was highly frustrated in the process. Little did I know that by being too determined (and anxious and angry at the previous physical therapist) that I was hindering my progress.

Finally the time came when they announced that I was done with physical therapy and there was nothing more they could do for me, even though my arm kept going numb in spots. In the meantime I had taken up running to keep physically fit. Not my idea of fun, but I was determined to baby step my way toward improving. I was able to baby step from not being able to run 10 steps without feeling like I was going to die, to participating in my first 5K two summers ago at the Woodstock Challenge.

But frequently, I'd be on the treadmill at the Y, overlooking the swimming pool and be praying, saying positive statements and being highly resentful that I couldn't swim. In fact, I had a bigger problem now. Not only was my previously injured arm/hand going numb frequently, but all of a sudden, my other arm started going numb, too. Terrifying. What the heck was going on?

PART 3 - TOO DETERMINED TO BE RELAXED?!?

Have you ever done research for a problem that doesn't go away, and you keep finding the same answers but they don't work? Ever had a nagging idea in the back of your mind that you discounted because it didn't make logical sense? I did. Nagging at me was something I had heard about massage therapy providing relieve for those suffering from long term tendinitis. Humph. I like doing things myself and didn't want to pay for an expensive massage that wouldn't work anyway. But I finally met a person who seemed qualified and trustworthy and made an appointment with her. Laura Kreassig at Back to Balance backtobalancestresscoaching.com/ worked with my tight, painful shoulder. At the end of the half hour session she asked, "So, how is your shoulder?" Startled, I thought, "What shoulder? It feels perfectly normal!!" Of course the numbness and tingling came back soon after, but I made another appointment with Laura. The second session she made some ridiculous comment like my "muscles had memory" or "there was an issue with my tissues". Being quite logical and a no nonsense gal, I jumped on those comments and said they made no sense to me. She explained a little bit and I asked her to email me with some information about it.

That started the process of learning to not be determined all the time, but to learn to relax. Aaarrrrggg! No, it's not the sound of Charlie Brown lying on the ground because Lucy took away the football he was going to kick. It's the sound of a logical, determined, hard working, constantly on the go and accomplishing things person trying to relax. It's really hard work.

If you're reading this, you are probably the hard working, get things done type (just making a logical assumption). You could be lying in a hammock, relaxing, reading this - but I doubt it. So what finally worked for me that just might work for you, too? Learning that my mind and body work together (not just the determined stuff I had been doing. "All right, body. Listen up. You're going to do 10,000 sit ups and you're going to like it!") Learning that my poor stressed mind can actually injure my body: it made the tendinitis last almost a year and a half, make my arms numb and painful, severely limited me in what I can actually physically do. Learning that I need to take time to meditate with Deepak Chopra, to try yoga, to breathe slowly and deeply, to read Martha Beck's books and implement what I have learned in my life.

What a life changing epiphany: learning to relax so that I can determinedly get everything done that I want to. (Okay, not really everything I want to. And truthfully it still does irk me to take 15-20 minutes out of a day to relax and do "nothing". How unproductive. Ahh, on the contrary, how unproductive not to...)

Today, I'm back to swimming, and am regularly swimming a mile two times each week. (Yes! I am a swimmer!) And I'm teaching swimming at the Lake Geneva YMCA. I love all my students, but one of my many favorites is a wonderful lady in her 50s who had been afraid of the water but was determined to learn to swim. We've had two lessons so far, and she's now floating and kicking on her own beautifully. There was a break in our lessons because she just learned that she has cancer. However, she's determined to continue her swimming lessons and we'll be getting together for her next lesson in a few days. I'm so proud of her...

About the author:

Dorothy Robin www.linkedin.com/in/dorothyrobin/ is passionate about people and helping them improve their lives.

Dorothy is currently President of the Crystal Clear Toastmasters Club www.crystalcleartoastmasters.org/ and invites you to stop in and visit our club to see how you can improve your speaking and leadership skills. Our club's motto is: Speaking of Fun!

She is also a swimming instructor for both private and group lessons at the Lake Geneva, WI YMCA www.glymca.com.

Unfamiliar Territory

By Martha C. Zavala

While I was growing up, few things I did satisfied my father, but it was a given that he would be proud if I graduated from high school and continued on to college. Both my parents emigrated from Mexico and did not have the resources to continue to higher education. They've always expressed how important education is and pushed me in the right direction even though I didn't always agree. Now, at twenty-five, I've come to realize that I've grown beyond the expectations of my parents and established my own. It wasn't always easy to envision my goals but I've had to dig deep in myself for the motivation that no one could give me.

In high school I did fairly well academically but not well enough to be considered for a scholarship so I entered my local community college. After only a semester, I moved to Twenty-Nine Palms, California, to be with my husband who had enlisted in the Marines Corps. I still had the determination to attend college but it was put off when I found out I was pregnant. The option of school was just a dream since my sole purpose then was to care for my family. After moving back to my hometown I was at a loss for what I really wanted in life.

My marriage was going through a time of transition, adjusting from a military lifestyle to civilian life. We were both unemployed and depending on our families until we could stabilize ourselves. It was a rough time financially and emotionally. We were both determined to move ahead and encouraged each other in our endeavors. My husband was able to find a position that would allow us to live on our own. I encouraged him to enroll in school and since then has completed his Associate in Applied Science. My path has been slower but I've never given up my passion to further my education.

I re-enrolled in school and took one course each semester while I tried my luck in different positions ranging from food service, receptionist to medical assistant. During this time, my sister-in-law encouraged me to apply for a secretarial position. She worked for the local school district and was happy there. I ignored her encouragement because I was set in my ways, wanted to stay in my current position.

At first, I was enjoying my job at the pediatricians' office but after a few weeks, it turned sour. My co-workers were not team players, I felt like they were looking out for themselves. After waking up, day after day, and dreading going to work I knew something needed to change. I finally applied for the secretary job that my sister-in-law had talked so much about, and was offered the position.

It turned out to be more than I could have hoped for. The middle school where I work is a close-knit community. I am amazed at the dedication the teachers have for their students, and how the staff goes beyond what is expected of them. The people I work with are passionate about their careers, from administrators, teachers, to the secretaries. It's truly an example of teamwork. My position gave me insight into the educational path I would continue and introduced me to a new passion in life I never thought possible.

I became immersed in what the students were reading. My eyes were opened to young adult novels and I became an avid reader. With my interest in literature increasing, the changes to my educational goals became clearer. I thought, "Why not teach?" It's the one profession where I can share my thirst for literature and still work in an environment I valued. I looked into what other courses I would need, with the exception of a few, I was on track for an Associate in Arts degree.

Meanwhile, my new passion for writing materialized one day when I opened a Microsoft Word document and began to type.

Words appeared in the document that I couldn't believe I created. It started with a couple of words, then a paragraph, then a page and more. The idea that I liked to write was so new to me. I realized I wanted to share what I was creating, and once I had something concrete I looked for writing groups in my area. I came across one at my local library called the Writing Circle.

I took the first pages I had ever written to my first meeting. I wasn't sure what to expect. I was nervous when I found out I would be reading out loud and would receive comments about my work. The other members went first and I was shocked at how well they expressed their ideas on paper. Their work was detailed and spoke volumes about their characters. In comparison, my work was simple and had no depth. I was intimidated. When I began reading, my cheeks burned and my voice didn't sound like my own, I kept thinking how awful it sounded. I was afraid to hear these strangers' opinions on the inner workings of my brain. I was fearful for no reason; everyone was very polite and gave me helpful critiques. I went home that night filled with a new sense of adventure and determination. Joining a group of people who were passionate about writing inspired me. I wanted to write and realized I could do it alongside a degree in English Education.

I know my parents are proud of how I have grown beyond their expectations. I have followed my passion and never lost the motivation to pursue my educational goal. The desire to work toward a goal is the first step in achieving it. Knowing what your future ambitions are does not come easily to many. In my case, I was afraid of getting off track by trying something outside of my comfort level. It's a scary idea to leave what is familiar but if your life is not filled with desire for what you are working for then, what's the point? Even when your days look bleak and you feel like there is not more to life, you could be in for a surprise. You will still come across obstacles and life changes, but the key to staying on course is not about settling for what you know; it's about the courage to stray away from it. Take chances and ignite your passion.

About the author:

Martha Zavala lives in the suburbs of Chicago with her husband and son. She's pursuing a BA in English Education. She reads anytime she has a free moment. She has a profound love for literature. Martha can be contacted via e-mail at: martha_c.zavala@yahoo.com.

PEARL: HER PERFECTLY IMPERFECT LIFE IGNITES MY PASSION

By Susan Schuerr

"There is no such thing as 'normal'. Normal is a setting on the dryer." Pearl Gannon

I received a phone call from the Northwest Herald last year saying that I was nominated to be one of the recipients of the Everyday Hero award. I was flattered to be recognized for my volunteer efforts in helping others, but I was doing what I am programmed to do. My passion is to help others achieve their goals in life. I love mentoring and connecting people.

If anyone is an Everyday Hero, it is my young friend Pearl. Even her name was rightly chosen. By definition a pearl is a precious thing---the finest example of something. Pearl Gannon has the loveliest smile as she looks up at me from her hand-cycle provided by Adaptive Adventures, an organization that provides sports activities for the disabled. Click---we have a picture taken of us as she prepares to bike in the North Shore Bike Tour held in Chicago in September.

This is her second bike ride----the first being Bike the Drive. She is a nationally recognized wheelchair athlete with passions for sports too numerous to mention. People are drawn to Pearl because of her upbeat personality, her tenacity and of course her changing hair color. Today her short curly hair is burgundy. The spunky 26 year old loves fashion especially an assortment of hats and flowing skirts.

I asked Pearl to share a little about her daily battle with Muscular Dystrophy---a disease she has had since she was 8 years old.

She went to public schools and had special accommodations, but did not need a wheel chair until after high school.

"I've really never let being in a wheelchair stop me," said Pearl. I've participated in basketball, softball, waterskiing, wake boarding and down-hill skiing." Her face lit up when she said, "I've even gone skydiving three times. I was the first physically disabled person the skydiving organization had ever worked with. The hardest part was stepping out of the plane to a free fall of 120 miles an hour. When the parachute opened, I was able to relax and forget for a moment about being disabled. The scenery was breathtakingly beautiful from my birds' eye view."

My husband belayed her while she rock climbed in the Illinois Palisades. She was one of the few who pulled herself up without assistance, an example of her tenacity.

Her life has been a series of ups and downs. As a child, her father hid her crutches on her thinking she was faking her disability. Her mother and three sisters have had a more positive and supportive role in her life. Pearl's involvement in athletic competitions has opened up her world. She enjoyed her numerous opportunities to travel to different states. In high school, her disability kept her from competing in sports. But she is certainly making up for lost time now having won the Most Valuable Player in basketball.

Pearl also talked about a dark period in her life when she was losing hope. When she weighed 85 pounds she was hospitalized for an eating disorder. "I really shouldn't be here," she said. "But the chaplain came to visit me every day during my 26 day stay." It was at this time she turned to God who gave her the strength to go on. Her latest disappointment was not being able to finish the track season this past summer due to complications of a feeding tube placement two weeks prior to competition. "I get upset when I don't feel comfortable wearing a bikini or specific shirts because I now have a feeding tube, and yet the feeding tube will give me the strength to be better at sports." She consumes 1300 calories while sleeping.

We went to lunch at her favorite restaurant, Olive Garden, where I interviewed her for this story. Across from me sat this beautiful young woman with a zest for life few of us have encountered. She has every excuse in the world to be depressed and down. But on the contrary, Pearl is going to make each day count. At twenty-six the doctors say she is as good as she is going to get. I am hoping she beats the odds and that she will achieve her dream of one day representing the USA in women's wheelchair basketball. She also is adamant about getting an education.

Pearl graduated with a grade point average of 4.9 out of 5.0 points from Glenbard East High School in Lombard, Illinois. She has a thirst for learning and is looking forward to obtaining a wheelchair accessible van so she can continue her education. "I still have not had the chance to finish my degree and that's one thing that's very important to me." A degree in Psychology would help her land a job working with people she understands, the disabled.

As you can see, Pearl ignites my passion. Here is a woman that has so much to deal with daily, but she rises above it all. Next time we get together, it will probably be at Starbucks where she loves to journal while sipping her favorite drink, Salted Caramel Hot Chocolate with extra salt. Here is an example of the advice she gives to others.

Pearl Gannon's Pearls of Wisdom

- My biggest piece of advice is there is no such thing as perfect. I have the hardest time accepting this myself, but it's something I need to remember and be reminded of.
- I love to be able to tell my story of what I've been through and overcome in life. You truly cannot help someone else out until you help yourself, so take your own advice, better yourself and then go on to help someone else.
- Lastly, and I think I struggle with this the most; there is no such thing as 'normal'. Normal is a setting on the dryer. Who describes what "normal" is anyway? Embrace not being normal.

About the author:

Susan Schuerr has been published in the Love Notes section of the Chicago Tribune, an anthology entitled *Falling in Love with You* and *Ignite Your Passion Kindle Your Internal Spark V1*. For more information, contact her at sschuerr@gmail.com and see her web site www.lifewithlarry.org. Susan Schuerr, an educator, writer and speaker, lives in Fox River Grove, Illinois with her husband, Larry. They have three grown children and five grandchildren. She is a member of Toastmasters International and Algonquin Area Writers Club. She taught English and Drama in District 155 and writes regularly for *Compassion and Justice* blog.

DOVE

By John J.W. Guanci, III
FOILED AGAIN...

Passion can be embodied in so many different ways, so many different manifestations of something that calls to our hearts in a bid to make us more than what we were prior to a given moment or a certain experience. A calling and a drive in pursuit of something we love.

But allow me the luxury of being quite clear, passion is that for which we are willing to suffer deeply as we are in pursuit of that which brings us to our feet with our head back and our eyes cast to the heavens. Standing, we are exhausted in the emotion of the outpouring from our inner being into an expression, a process that changes us forever and by the grace of God will touch the lives of others in a meaningful way.

One of my keystone passions in life is that of words and how they are linked to form wisdom. That all too precious meeting of hindsight and foresight. It is a greater thrill when these moments come not from hours of study or contemplation, but rather come straight out of the blue and from a source one might not expect. Like a bolt of lightning riding on the back of inspiration, captured in a flash of insight.

To that end, one might spend a few hours reading a portion of a great literary work and then contemplate, for comparatively extended periods of time, how that tome overlays the content and the standing of one's own life. Gleaning relevant insight from something that was written by another person from another generation, or even another century is comforting and inspiring. Much in the way traditions of nobility and the ways of dignified behavior are comforting and inspiring. For they envelope our senses and provide a guide light by which we can walk through a world that clearly is in need of this and so much more.

What of those times when we are truly inspired and words, in their purest expression fall upon the shoulders of our unsuspecting minds and so gently land that we cannot help but pay attention to their sincerity. That it is not the great composition of words or works from some "master," but rather it comes from a writing which is meant for a very different purpose.

In a moment such as this I am at my best and my heart takes flight. For what is assembled in the way of thought, the connections made are mine and mine alone. Being inspired by the words of others is magnificent and to stand on the shoulders of thought is an honor, unique to the human race and all of mankind. But to take away wisdom, having laid the foundation and the bricks myself while inviting others to stand upon them, that my dear friends is a calling that brings me closer to the sweet rhythm of my own heartbeat than almost anything else in this world.

Recently there was such a time when I was going about a most regular task, one that I enjoy thoroughly and to my core. I was eating a piece of dark chocolate. As I sat there, enjoying that delectable morsel I found it pale in comparison to the three words I found on the wrapper that had just recently encased this fine and sweet delicacy. For as I smoothed out the foil the red words became clear. Drawing them nearer the glow of a single light bulb that blazed in the darkness of my office I read them aloud: "Engage, Embrace, Enjoy."

I read them again, a bit slower, almost as if to indicate deep contemplation, "Engage, Embrace, Enjoy."

Sitting there thinking, what do these three words truly mean? Do they act as pillars of thought which support clearly a higher concept or ideal? They were, after all, simple words on a foil wrapper…it is important not to read too much into it. This is true; do not read too much into it, read everything into it! I continued, what do these words mean to one another? How is their being together a greater result than them being alone merely hanging in space? How do these three simple words, which were clearly pop culture's attempt at influencing my emotional response to a product, work together to create wisdom in my life and, God willing, in the lives of others?

The words were correct but the order was just a bit out of sorts, tumblers placed in a given combination let people into an unlocked space where, in the case of words, there is treasure to be found, riches to be had and wealth to be shared.

Again, those three words, reordered, are: engage, embrace and enjoy.

When we engage we are positively connected to the moments that construct our lives. Visions of mechanical connections come to mind, for if our life is a journey then to engage is the process by which we are converting the power of who we are into forward progress. Much like a transmission does with an engine. Without the practical matter of being engaged, of transferring our thoughts, our hopes and our ambitions into action, we are destined to sit by the side of the road at redline going nowhere fast. More unfortunate is the fact that so many sit with visions of the wind mussing their hair, while in reality, it all remains neatly parted.

But with such a concrete and visual analogy I concede readily that there is quite a bit of abstraction present. After all, what exactly is a moment anyway? It is a word that is used far too often and to a point where the value of its commodity has been cheapened and commonplace. So within this space allow me the luxury of defining what a moment happens to be and then, the texture, of being engaged in one will come to the fore.

A moment, it is longer than a second, yet, it is quite a bit shorter than a minute. It is that which is unique unto you and to you alone. For within that same point-in-time, as experienced by a number of different people, you will all share the space but each extract a different moment. It is the perceptive fingerprint of your very soul and it seen through the lenses of experience, belief and attitudes. This word, moment, is the time it takes your heart to beat one time.

We know, at least we should, we have no promise of tomorrow or even the promise of the next ten minutes. We should have little confidence in anything but our current heartbeat. So in our lives we are to be engaged in this, for we have no promise of another. To move down the road trip of our existence in pursuit of self-interests and to relish in the opportunity to benefit the lives of others by the thoughts we manifest via the words we use and the actions we take. To meet the needs of others, simply and plainly, as those needs meets us. To not turn away, but to stare back unflinching and engage in the moment of making our lives better by voluntarily enhancing the lives of others.

The second word is embracing. Embracing is a word that brings about many a pleasant thought and a grand collection of memories. When we embrace something we are holding it close to our core, pulling it tight and not wanting to let go. Likewise we hold that idea, memory or person a little closer to thee so the experience can become a part of who we are as individuals. Perhaps to just tease ourselves, just a bit with the idea of remaining there, in the moment, forever.

Personally, I have been blessed by God with a few truly amazing relationships. One of those was with my Grandpa. I can picture those times when I would hug my Grandpa as a child and as an adult before leaving for home. I did not want to let go and I did not want to say goodbye. It was the kind of wanting that did not bring about a smile, but that which was so deep and important that I remember grimacing because I knew I would have to let go at some point. There was nothing about him that made me want to part his side, the smell of Vitalis or Lucky Strike cigarettes, all of it a golden memory and there isn't a single day during which I don't wish I could have that experience just one more time. To have held on for just a little while longer. This process of embracing is a rewarding one, it brings hope to our hearts and we cherish them so.

Again, it is no different with ideas or the notions that swirl within us every single day. There are those that make us very comfortable, very much at ease and so very warm inside. A time when victory was ours, love was in the air and nothing could possibly go wrong as God was in His heaven and all was right with the world…contentment and deep rooted joy abounded.

For what of those memories and personal accounts that may not have been so glorious or so abundantly pleasant? When we were not at our best and others knew it, when we were, quite possibly, at our worst and still, others knew it. Actions and behaviors that we would rather repress to the far reaches of our mind or some other far off land mass or continent, banished and in exile never to return the present day as a reminder of our humanity.

Our failures are a part of who we are and regardless as to how hard we try to push them away emotionally they can never leave our side. So in this way when we do not embrace the bad and the difficult times of our lives there is this conflict between what we want, driven by our ego, and what we actually have, presented by the stark contrast of our reality. In this way, why should we expend the effort to be rid of something that cannot be purged?

Admittedly, this is where the lifting becomes a bit heavier. We must embrace our worst moments and hold them close to our bosom, right next to our heartbeat as a reminder and as guidance. Guidance for what we do not what to become, how we do not want to conduct ourselves or for results we do not desire. As much as success and triumph motivate and encourage it is failure and heartbreak, upon reflection, that teaches and imparts wisdom.

This bring us to the last word, enjoy. I don't know of anyone whose goal it is to not enjoy themselves, but it appears we mistake the word enjoy (to be in-joy) with happiness. Happiness is a new car with bright red paint; standing slack-jawed in the moment as we bounce around emotionally. Enjoy, rather is appreciating and admiring that same car when it has 150,000 miles, a few scratches, a couple squeaks and more memories than we can count. Driven by how it has served us well and the value, via the quality of the "relationship", it has brought to our lives. Happiness, is tantamount to infatuation whereas the word enjoy is joined at the hip with enduring love.

Along those same lines, our last word appears to clearly have associated with it a value-added proposition with regards to our activities. That said, in order to enjoy one's life it is my opinion that ours has to be one of substance and of significance. Woe to the person who simply wants to swing from shallow vine to shallow vine like some "Good-Time-Charlie," eventually the sugar rush of happy moments runs out and we are only left with the reality of having done nothing real with the time we have been afforded.

The question that always begs asking is, how do we enjoy our lives? Can such a formula be extracted from the core of life's wellspring of experiences, let alone a chocolate wrapper?

Yes, for us to enjoy, to truly revel in and enjoy our lives we must engage the moment and we must embrace the totality of who we are, good and bad, as people. As we engage the moment, positively connect in the span of time it takes our heart to beat just once, we have the opportunity to bring elements of beauty, intelligence and assistance to the lives of those around us.

This process brings to our own lives a richer context as we extend beyond our internal focus and look outward to a world, to a person, who needs our assistance. That we, by our actions, might leave our fingerprint on the lives of others as we intentionally act in a way, which will bring them benefit and uplift their moment in time as defined by their heartbeat.

However, this is only possible if we take the time to embrace all of whom we are, learning via reflection upon our mistakes, developing wisdom. There is never a situation where a person can give away what it is they do not personally own for themselves. To extract the richest pearls of wisdom takes work, patience and an effort motivated by a deep desire to understand. To not run from, but to wrestle with, our background as people because of who we want to become, what we want to be about as we meet the needs as the needs meet us.

Putting it all together: we engage in the moment, which is our heartbeat, with wisdom that has been achieved through reflection, as we embrace who we are, and enjoy the process of living because we are adding value to the lives of other people.

Sweet are the morsels that come concealed in foil wrappers with a message inside; those that melt at the slightest provocation. But that they so pale by comparison to the sweet nature of words that by their content and context have the ability to melt our hearts as we discover that for which we feel deep and genuine passion. The embodiment of not just who we are, but action surrounding who we want to become, identifying that for which we are ever so willing to suffer deeply.

About the author:

John J.W. Guanci, III is the Owner/Wordsmith of Beyond Rhetoric and wholly dedicated to enriching and improving organizational health and communications by applying the leadership concepts of John Maxwell. Keying on the notion that the only way to change the space around us is to change what dwells inside of us. With nearly 20 years of managerial and executive experience, John not only possesses insight to business relationships; he also possesses great levels of empathy and understanding. Contact him at john@beyond-rhetoric.com.

Doing the Right Thing

By Bill Koza

Some of you may have watched the TV series Friday Night Lights. I happen to enjoy this show, but not because of the reasons you might think. Aside from the compelling story lines and positive message of each program, I like it because it's about a high school football coach. You see, my father-in-law was a high school football coach as well. You've probably never heard of him, but you may have heard of the town in which he coached, Eureka, IL. He also coached the football team for Eureka College, President Ronald Reagan's alma mater. His name Warner McCollum and they called him Coach Mac.

Although he was my father-in-law, I had no idea how deeply he inspired a generation of kids, now adults, as the high school football coach. That is until a few years ago at his memorial service. It was at his memorial service that I discovered what a truly remarkable person Coach Mac was.

Eureka is a small town in central Illinois. You might have missed it on your way to Peoria since it has only one stoplight. But at Coach Mac's memorial service, over 300 people attended from eight states.

As part of the service, some of his former players had a chance to speak. One person told the story of how Coach Mac lived his life with integrity and always "did the right thing." He went on to say that Coach Mac really hated seeing high school football scores such as 40-14 or 36-0. He thought such lopsided scores proved nothing. During one game, Coach Mac's team was winning and clearly dominating. At this point, Coach called a time out to talk to the quarterback on the sideline. He told the quarterback, "I don't want you scoring another point." Confused, the quarterback said,

"What? I can't tell the team not to score any points!" Coach Mac said, "Yes you can, and you will." He said, "I know that man on the other side of the field, he is good man, and I am not going to do that to him or his team." They went on to finish the game and win, and afterwards the quarterback came to Coach Mac and asked him why he did what he did. Coach Mac said, "Because it was the right thing to do."

Coach Mac believed that high school or grade-school football was more than winning a game. He believed that the kids would not remember a game where they blew out the opponent; rather they would remember playing the game. He coached with the aim of teaching the kids lessons that were more meaningful and that they could take with them then apply throughout their life.

Besides the technical lessons of playing football he focused on lessons such as drive, self-determination, integrity, sportsmanship and trust. The fact that the players who spoke at Coach Mac's memorial service were from the class of '66 is a testament to his long-term impact and speaks volumes to the power of how he treated people.

Later that evening after the memorial service another person, who did not have chance to speak, came up to my wife and gave her a big hug and offered his condolences. He wanted her know how her father profoundly changed his life, literally. He explained that he had developed cancer. He said that he remembered the lessons Coach Mac taught him. He had moved to Colorado by then, but he kept in touch with Coach Mac. He explained that it was what Coach Mac had taught him about himself that allowed him to get through his cancer. His cancer is in remission, and he credits Coach Mac for saving his life.

So the next time you are faced with doing the right thing, even when you are having a bad day, or when people don't understand why, I hope you remember this story about Coach Mac, because you never know how you might impact someone for the rest of their life.

The stories of Coach Mac changed me forever. The spirit of Coach Mac's ideas can live on in each of us by doing what we know is the right thing to do. By his standards, I have a long way to go. By the way, the next time you are near Eureka, Illinois, stop by the high school, walk out on the football field and look up at the scoreboard. You will a sign that says McCollum Field.

About the author:

Bill Koza is currently the Vice President of Emerging Business in a multi-million dollar international business. He has worked in companies of all sizes, from Xerox Corporation to a family owned retail store. He has a Bachelor's degree in Human Resources Management from DePaul University and specializes in leadership, strategy development and business plan development. Visit his website at www.boss-talk.com for leadership development articles and training.

THE CALL

Doug Elwell

When I was a kid, I sat with Mother in church on Sunday mornings and listened to Reverend Wallop sermonize about "answering the call". It was a thread that ran through most of his sermons and my childhood. He said God might call me to the cloth, to serve the Lord and if it came, it would be without warning, a bolt out of the blue and there was nothing I could do about it. That bothered me when I was twelve because even then I was pretty sure I didn't want to be called to the cloth. It was like when you're in school and the teacher called on you to recite and you were not prepared. I felt like that about His call.

But it didn't come. I managed to sneak into high school without it, yet the threat of it I'd lived with for years was still there. It hung over my head like the sword of Damocles until Mr. Finny came along. He changed all that and relieved me of my fear of an imminent call from You Know Who. Mr. Finny was an unlikely competitor to God in the matter of the call but very early on, as I got to know him, it was his call to teaching that I answered. It came before God's and I was sorely relieved.

Much later, when I thought about it, I realized my calling was metaphor for passion. I knew what I wanted to dedicate my life to. Thank God! Now if He called to offer me a position I could tell him I'd already accepted another offer, but thanks for considering me anyway.

I pursued my passion and graduated from university in the spring of 1971 with a high grade point average, a shiny new teacher's certificate and state of the art resume. I would have been a good hire and was confident someone out there would snatch me up as fast as they could. I sent scads of letters of inquiry to schools all over the state with no luck—not even an interview. In those days it was a buyer's market glutted with credentials like mine. Getting a teaching position was like trying to get a job with the city—ya gotta have a connection and I didn't have no connections.

Anyway, there I sat with a wife, a toddler son and a daughter on the way and no prospects. I began to doubt—had I answered the wrong call? Should I sit by the phone and wait for His call, one I didn't want to have to answer? The pressure was on so I beat a strategic retreat and applied to graduate school and took a Masters of Science in instructional technology. It kept me in the education field—close to teaching so I went for it. If I could just get my foot in the door, perhaps I could land a teaching position from within. My passion for teaching took a hit on the chin, but I was far from down for the count.

Passion thwarted? Hardly. In the early years of my career I often rethought my situation. I found I was getting satisfaction in my field. Work in a collegial environment that included not only teachers and administrators, but also students turned out to be my true calling. Instructional technology was rapidly evolving. It demanded constant adaptation not only to the technology itself, but also in designing classroom instruction to meet student and teacher needs.

For me, those challenges were demanding and rewarding. I thrived on them. Sometimes pursuing one's passion gets thwarted by factors that are beyond control, but I realized it wasn't necessarily the end of the world. When that happens, take a look inward, search for other possibilities that ignite your passion, what it is that makes you want to jump out of bed every morning and go to work. You may have to let go of old rubrics, reinvent yourself professionally, but rekindling your passion can be a good thing.

A quick word about technology. It happened to be my field, but today, unless you're making mud pies down by the river for a living, technology is integral to almost every profession. There it is, all dolled up in a slinky little black thing with spaghetti straps to seduce everyone into getting all caught up in the "gee-whiz" of it. We're human. We easily get distracted by all the gewgaws of the latest thing that comes along. Of course what it can do is important, but how best to apply it to achieve our mission is another matter. It's really the most important aspect of new and emerging technologies. The flash and dash of the latest "thing" to come down the pike too often takes our eye off the ball. Like the seductress it is, it misdirects.

In my profession, writing objectives to accomplish desirable outcomes then assessing the potential of the latest "thing" to see how it can be applied to meet those objectives isn't sexy, but it is the key to the whole process of harnessing the technology to best achieve any businesses' objectives. This is a long sentence, but it defines my passion. The beauty of it is that a variation of it can be applied to any field of endeavor. Just don't get seduced by the "gee-whiz" of it. There is a better way.

When I was in graduate school in the early seventies, the director of my program was fond of reminding us that we were in the people business. In addition to that he admonished us to forget the nuts and bolts of the technology. There will always be technicians to change a projector bulb or defrag your hard drive. We were training to do instructional design that included figuring out how to apply the technology to greatest effect. That was the fun part, my passion.

The notion of being in the people business was new to me then, but the concept was not. I recently read a column by I.F. Stone dating all the way back to December 1949. He was reporting on a meeting of an association in New York where, by his observation, the attendees were busily "making 'contacts', the American way of 'getting ahead,' whether in soap or science."[1] For those who don't remember December 1949, more recently Howard Schultz, founder and CEO of Starbucks famously said, "We are not in the coffee business serving people, but in the people business serving coffee."[2] This is a more eloquent statement of what was being said back in the forties and seventies, but you get the drift. Regardless of your field, you will always be swimming in a steady stream of technology. Re-word Shultz's mantra to say: We are not in the business of using people to serve technology, but using technology to serve people. 'Nuff said about technology.

So what are the take-aways here? How does all this relate to igniting your passion? Regardless of your field, these points are applicable precisely because there are truths imbedded in them that each generation in the work force needs to relearn. So I learned a few things about passion along the winding road that was my career:

Gaze at your navel once in a while. Reflect occasionally on what it is that gets you out of bed in the morning. You might find your passion has, or is flagging. It isn't necessarily a static thing. Don't let it burn down like an untended campfire to leave you sitting with a plate of cold beans in the chill of a dark night.

Beware sexy, glitzy baubles that come along. Too often they misdirect. It's the old "keep your eye on the ball" thing. Business, like education, is too often quick to jump on the latest bandwagon that comes along. Be skeptical of bandwagon descriptors like "new" and "scientific" and "research shows". New? Scientific? Maybe. Maybe not. Someone once said about stories, if they're good they're not new and if they're new they're not good. (This story is a perfect example. It's not new, but it's good.) I'm not one to throw a shoe into the machinery, but think about it—more often than not bandwagons turn out to be just that. They make a lot of noise for about fifteen minutes then fade quickly as soon as they are found out for what they are. Remember 8-track tapes? As Solomon, in his wisdom, said, "Nothing under the sun is new."

Unless you live alone in an old beat up eight wide somewhere in the New Mexico desert and live off mule deer venison and your only company are rattle snakes and kangaroo mice, no matter what your field, you are, and always will be, in the people business. "Plays well with others" is good to have on a resume. Unlike bandwagons, it is a constant. "Plays well with others" won't ever break down and run off the road to litter the shoulders with all the other broken down abandoned bandwagons that came and went like that pile of 8-track tapes over there.

Have the courage to embrace your changing passion when you sense it is flagging. Redefine it. Life is too short to moil away at something for years only to find that you've lost the once hot passion for your career that drove you to rip its clothes off in the middle of the night. I know it's easy to say and hard to do. Mid-career car payments, the mortgage, upcoming college expenses, that trip to Key West you've always wanted to take can make you feel trapped. But there are stories every day of folks who reinvent themselves and find deep happiness and personal satisfaction for taking that step to merge onto another career path. Your husband or wife, maybe your kids and possibly even your in-laws will still love you.

When that call comes, catch it on the first ring.

1. Stone, I.F., *The Truman Era*. (New York: Vintage Books, 1973) 145.
2. Read, Catherine S. *"We're in the People Business."* Social Media Strategy, Twitter. Creative Read, Inc. (August 31, 2009) 1p. online, Internet, 29 Apr, 2013.

This is a work of creative nonfiction. Some names, characters, places, dialog or descriptions have been changed or added. In those cases, any resemblance to actual events or locales or persons, living or dead, is entirely coincidental.

About the author:
Doug Elwell was born in Chicago, Illinois and raised on the prairie in rural downstate where he spent his formative years. He explores the influences of place and community in our lives through creative non-fiction and fiction short stories. His work has appeared in The Oakland Independent, the first edition of *Ignite Your Passion: Kindle Your Inner Spark, True Stories Well Told, Every*

Writer's Resource and *Midwestern Gothic*. Doug can be contacted via email at djelwell@mchsi.com.

A Balloon Lady's Guide to a Passionate Life

By Holly Nagel

Often our road towards self-preservation leads us down uncertain paths. For some, overcoming great adversity means knowing fearlessness by taking risks and being able to laugh at yourself along the way.

Chaos to Clown Shoes and Beyond!

>Me: "What's your favorite thing to do in the whole wide world?"

>Six year old girl: "Laugh!"

Making a living as a balloon lady was not something I would have guessed I would be doing as an adult, not in a million years. Then I was faced with a series of challenges and nothing has been the same since.

Once my life was full of crises. Not just one crisis. But many crises.

The loose interpretation for the Chinese pictogram 'crisis' is 'danger' plus 'opportunity,' and at that point in my life I felt plenty of danger, however I did not see much opportunity.

Were you ever in a very challenging place in life? Well, not only was my living room ceiling leaking, but my toddler was being mistreated in preschool; I was on the verge of being fired from my full time job; my father had a terminal illness; his house burned down; even the family dog died.

And in that time of crises, do you know what I did? I did what any other red-blooded American woman would do. I went back to school and took a class. I took a clown class! I definitely needed the emotional break and silliness.

Upon completion of the clown class, we all had created our own unique face, we had professional looking costumes and I even had custom made clown shoes. These were red and white leather beauties. About two-feet long. Snazzy! Can you imagine walking in them? I am five-foot-one, can you imagine me walking in them?

I loved wearing them. I wore them around the house. I wore them to get the mail. Then the time came when I could wear them professionally. It was at a parade. My clown club, or alley, would participate entertaining in parades throughout the summer and I realized I could break in my snazzy new shoes!

At the staging area of most parades, there would be the line of single-size portable potties. Per usual, before absolutely anything in my life could begin, I would first have to go. And being at this parade was no exception.

So, I stood in the long line with my long shoes, yukking it up with everyone around me. It was a perfect summer morning, so the waiting was not so bad.

Finally, a potty was available.

I bounded over, jumped in, and gave the door a yank. And a yank. And a yank, yank, yank. The door would not close. My shoes were too long. With my frustration mounting, I tried turning my feet every which way, including parallel with the potty itself. And all this while trying desperately not touch anything.

I still could not shut the door. I heard the people in line behind me start to laugh. And laugh. All the folks waiting in line thought this was part of my shtick, or my clown act. It turns out I was providing some comic relief to their waiting, but there was no relief for me that morning.

STRETCH AND BE FLEXIBLE!

>Child: "Balloon lady! Balloon lady!"
>
>Dad: "Honey her name is Holly. You can call her Holly."
>
>Child: "Okay Daddy, but her name is Balloon Lady!"

As my son's third birthday approached I thought, "What perfect timing!" I could try out my new clown skills at his party. Word spread and different moms started hiring me to entertain at their own family events. As my popularity grew so did my business. I created promo materials like handmade business cards and flyers then brought them, along with a bunch of balloon sculptures, to local businesses.

It was not long before I received the big phone call from an amusement park offering to pay me a handsome sum for a week of my balloon work. My husband and I looked at each other, eyebrows raised in disbelief, wondering aloud at the fantastic possibilities with this new endeavor. By paying attention to this one seemingly crazy opportunity my life began to change.

It is a known fact that stretching out our muscles before participating in a physical activity reduces the chance of muscle strains and injury and increases the chances we will have an enjoyable experience. So it is with balloons, since a brittle balloon quite simply will burst. And so it is with our personal and professional growth. If we do not customarily flex and open ourselves to new ideas, we risk missing the opportunity to something better.

Compared to where I was months earlier, my spirits were definitely lifted at my new prospects. By stretching my worldview, being flexible and taking a chance, I popped all previous notions about what I was supposed to do. Just letting it all go. Only then was I was truly able to grow and rise to the new challenges that presented themselves.

Previously, I did not think being flexible was a good trait at all. I thought it conveyed weakness and indecisiveness. A wishy-washiness, if you will. However, I learned flexibility actually allowed for my transformation to occur.

Where There's a Leak, There's a Lesson!

> Eight year old boy: Wow! That's super! And you didn't even know what you were doing!"

I did learned three things after entertaining at that first event as a clown that reinforced my decision to stop clowning. I could not do magic tricks. I could not juggle. But I sure could make a balloon dog! I realized being a clown was not for me and I wanted it to work out very much. I loved being entertained by them, I just was not completely comfortable being a clown myself.

So, I got rid of my wig, costume and even my beloved clown shoes. Yes, money was spent and it was not an easy decision, however golden nuggets were certainly gleaned.

It is not a bad thing to be able to say, "You know what? I learned a lesson here and have to discontinue this now." To be able to know when something just is not right for you any longer is a crucial element to continuing your own evolution and developing a real awareness of where your own passions lie. Stop wasting your time and energy trying to make things work out when you are actually being drained by it, even in small amounts. Sometimes quitting something can be the best thing you do.

I decided to focus solely on balloon art in all its forms. In addition, I wanted to set myself apart. After all, there was apparently something about me that got a program director at a national amusement park to notice me and hire me for a weeklong event. I even asked and he replied he had actually waited in line with his young daughter for 45 minutes in order to receive a balloon sculpture from me. While waiting, he had a lot of time to watch how I conducted myself, observe how I interacted with everyone and decide I would be a good fit for his event.

What a revelation. Something about me! I thought I was only making balloon animals for the children, not communicating to others in any way. I felt pretty dumb. Now it all seemed so obvious. I am a slow learner, but once I catch on, watch out! I began thinking long and hard about my various qualities. I even asked family and friends what they thought my strengths and weaknesses were. Then I began paying attention to what clients and colleagues were telling me. Combine all that with reading various self help books and using other self help tools I started to take a real inventory of my gifts.

Taking the customer service and entertainment knowledge I already had, I began what would end up being years of research into the various components that were involved in making a great impression. After all, if I was entertaining people by creating balloon art for a long line, I did not have much time with each person as their turn came up to communicate much, but I did have time to make a big nonverbal impact while those waiting in line watched me.

WHERE THERE'S A LEAK, THERE'S A LAUGH! (AND A SOLUTION!)

> Two sisters with distinct southern accents. Little sister laughing because my electric pump sounds funny.
>
> Big Sister: "Why are you laughing?"
>
> Little Sis: "Because her machine made a farting sound!"
>
> Big Sis: "Don't say fart, say pass gas. It's nicer!"
>
> Turning to me she states matter-of-factly: "My Daddy passes gas in Georgia"

Leaks Happen.

Like the time I pulled up to the office complex for a delivery of several bouquets only to open the door and whoosh! Out of my vehicle the balloons were gone with the wind.

Or the time I delivered dozens of centerpieces to my client only to find major deflations occurring while I am setting them up on their tables, with client and staff all around.

Or the time I was installing for an outdoor event with a celebrity event planner and the landscapers would accidentally pop my ground level décor with their weed wackers.

What did I do? Did I throw myself onto the floor and have a big fat meltdown? You can bet I sure wanted to! Instead my years as a journalist, as an entertainer and as a decorator have provided me with what I call my SDS, that is, my Sweet Duckie Skills. A smile widens across my face and on the surface I am all smooth sailing and in control. Underneath I am paddling like heck!

Fortunately, I learned from the wisdom and mistakes of others to always carry enough balloons to re-create anything whenever I would make a delivery or installation. To date, I have only had to use my emergency balloons several times. By being proactive, or solutions oriented, I would take all the possible precautions including even pre-making sculptures hours or days in advance to double check for leaks. I still cannot predict all the leaks, pops and other surprises that are going to happen, but when they occur, at least I know I have done all I could to prevent or correct troubles.

Being able to react to problems calmly and effectively when they arise is great, but sometimes we do not have certain resources available to us to respond effectively. When we are solution oriented or proactive, we are better able to identify the root of the problems and difficulties. It can be as simple as leaving earlier. Not allowing enough driving time was a problem of mine for some time, until I finally got so tired of white-knuckling my steering wheel I decided to leave earlier. That means I always leave earlier, because I learned I would rather have extra time than the stress of running late. Or bringing an extra inflator, because I learned my main pump may possibly break and indeed has. Sometimes we can anticipate problems then when we are able to identify them clearly as they occur, we can decide if we need to go through it, under it, over it or around it.

Often I debrief myself after an event, especially if it was particularly unusual, customized or large. I may even add some notes to a design or in my journal of things I may do differently in the future. We all have our moments of hindsight being so much better than foresight. Those thoughts of I-Coulda-Shoulda-Woulda! But do not get carried away with all those shoulds. Afterwards, I remind myself to let it all go with the last knot and it is a helpful way to move on.

Balloons are Special and so are You!

> Mother of a seven year old boy: "He's had a new wallet for months, but he won't put anything in it except one thing. Your business card!"

I decided to offer balloon entertainment, balloon deliveries, balloon exhibits and balloon storytelling. Tiny balloons and grand installations. Balloons to wear and balloons to hold. Plus, I love using metaphors and balloons lend themselves to all kinds. Leaks happen. Pop your perceptions. Inflate your expectations. And on and on!

The balloon business is definitely not for the meek. The very nature of balloons defies logic and goes straight for the heart.

Remember the story of *Winnie the Pooh and a Day for Eeyore*? In it, Pooh plans to bring Eeyore a gift of a pot of honey, but does not get far, as he gets hungry and eats all the honey. He is left with an empty pot. Meanwhile, Piglet has a lovely red balloon he is going to give Eeyore, but he trips and accidentally bursts the balloon. The two friends meet to give Eeyore the gifts and Eeyore loves them because he can put his broken balloon into the empty pot, which he does over and over again.

Or witness the child who continues to hang on to the balloon long after it has worn out its recognizability. I think it is all about heart and the feeling in which it was given. In fact, whether a balloon sculpture consists of two balloons or 20, I believe it is all about the spirit of a balloon.

Rise to Your Brilliance

Through a series of events I ended up living a life and making a living in life by doing some of my favorite things. I did not plan all this. Who could? I like to say I have been blessed to be able to live a life that is delightful, delicious and deliberate. It all grew out of combined desires, goals and priorities. As well as being open to the possibilities that are out there. And more importantly, within myself.

I hope you, too, will be open to your gifts. Involve yourself. Identify them. Own them. You are already living a passionate life.

About the author:

In elementary school **Holly Nagel** got in trouble for her chatty ways. Sent to the back of the classroom, she always managed to make new friends there, too. Hollyism: Never underestimate the supposed weaknesses of youth, sometimes they become our greatest attributes later in life! Now, she connects people, one balloon at a time, with professional speaking and training programs, specializing in nonverbal communication and making a great impression. Visit her at www.HollyNagel.com.

USING SOCIAL NETWORKING TO SAVE LIVES

By Alexis Williams

Have you ever felt so utterly compelled to help someone or something in need? The urge pulls and tugs at your heart to do something that can help something that is almost helpless on their own. This is how I feel when it comes to animals. Today, there are more organizations than ever that are dedicated to helping and saving the lives of our furry friends.

Those efforts, while they make a big impact compared to 20 years ago, are still not enough. Every year there are hundreds of thousands of animals that are euthanized and/or abused by humans. This fact breaks my heart and tugs at my emotions, as there is nothing that I can do to save all of these helpless animals. There are however things that I can do to help make an impact.

Instead of standing by with the knowledge that these things are happening, this where I chose to take actions to bring down the numbers of animals being euthanized and/or being abused. In hearing about my interest in volunteering at a local animal welfare organization, my coworker told me about Animal House Shelter in Huntley, Illinois. I had expressed interest in making a difference in animals' lives and volunteering with a local organization. Through my research I had found that most of the large animal advocate organizations only use a fraction of their donations towards helping animals that are homeless or in need.

My coworker's close friend, Lesley Irwin, established Animal House Shelter in 2002 originally out of Barrington, Illinois. As the organization grew larger and they found themselves taking in more animals, they saw the need for a larger facility. Animal House Shelter later moved out to Huntley, Illinois where their current facility can temporarily house up to 300 cats and dogs while they await new homes.

Finding new homes for homeless cats and dogs is no easy task. It takes many volunteers, employees and lots of awareness for a homeless animal to find a new home. Many homeless animals spend months or years in an animal shelter, awaiting a new home and family. Some are not as lucky and are euthanized due to a lack of room to house them in the animal shelter. Animal House Shelter is a no-kill shelter, where they will not euthanize an animal due to lack of room. To combat the hurdle of not having enough room as well as continually bringing in more animals whom would be euthanized if not rescued, Animal House Shelter relies on many foster families who will temporarily take an animal in while the shelter is looking for a new home and family for the animal.

When you volunteer at Animal House Shelter's facility, there are a number of tasks or jobs you can take on. My first experience volunteering there, I opted to help greet possible adopters in the lobby. I welcomed the potential adopters and held dogs while the staff went into the back of the shelter to bring certain animals to the front for the potential adopters to meet. I love that Animal House Shelter operates this way. It prevents additional stress on the dogs by only having the staff allowed access the kennels where the dogs are housed.

I was new to volunteering at an animal shelter so I offered to do whatever was needed. Soon I found an eight-pound, brownish, mangy looking dog in my lap. One of the staff members asked me to hold her while they brought out a different dog for the potential adopter to meet. As this dog sat in my lap and snuggled into my arms, it was clear that all she wanted was a home and a family to love her. This tiny dog had made an imprint in my heart. The next time I went back to volunteer, I asked if she was still at the shelter. I learned her name was Bumpkin. She was still at the shelter and I asked to play with her for a while. That day I fell in love with her and knew I had to have her. I already had a four-year-old Jack

Russell Terrier and a one-year-old Miniature Pinscher at home. What was one more? On Easter Sunday that year, I went back to the shelter and brought Bumpkin home to live with me for good. This might have been the day where I turned my love for dogs into a passion for animals.

I continued stopping at the shelter every now and then to volunteer, but found that I was very tempted to bring home all the dogs and cats there when I volunteered. Instead, I asked the owner of the shelter, Lesley, if there were volunteer activities I could help with outside of the shelter. With enthusiasm she said, "Of course!"

It was then that I soon began helping with events that sponsored the animal shelter, held outside of the shelter. I was excited to see the participation from the public and the funds that these events were generating to help all of these homeless animals.

At this time, Facebook was gaining popularity not only with people but also with organizations. Seeing an opportunity to gain some free awareness with the public, I asked Lesley if it was okay to set up a group on Facebook for the animal shelter. She was excited about the opportunity and told me to go for it. I eagerly set up a new group on Facebook for people with an interest in Animal House Shelter. Before we knew it we had a couple hundred people who had joined the Facebook group.

Facebook evolved and we had an opportunity to convert the group to fans of a Facebook Page for organizations. The Facebook Page provided much more functionality than the group site offered so we made the transition. It was a slow migration but over a few years we now have more than 7,800 Facebook Page fans! While this may not seem like a large number of fans, for a small no-kill shelter in the suburbs, this is an impressive number!

For Animal House Shelter, Facebook is used everyday to communicate numerous things. From supplies the shelter needs, to animals who need transportation, to the great news that one of the animals has been adopted. This communications vehicle has become a fabulous way of engaging with the public and helping the animals, without costing the shelter anything but willing volunteers time. In addition, we found that our Facebook Page establishes opportunities for other animal welfare organizations to cross post about animals in need and communicate when dire circumstances arise. We help connect those in the community who also care about animals, while finding another vehicle to help find the homeless animals new families and homes. This is truly the power of technology and a love for animals at work!

There are so many things that animals do for humans that humans do not often do without requiring something in return. Often, humans expect compensation for things that they do; whether it is money, services or recognition. But just think of what animals provide us with everyday without expecting to be reimbursement. From a family pet, to service dogs, to bomb-sniffing dogs, not only do they provide us with protection, they also provide us with love, comfort and company. These are only a few reasons that I am so incredibly passionate about taking care of these creatures and being an advocate against their homelessness and abuse.

About the author:

By trade **Alexis Williams** is an e-commerce and marketing professional. Her other passions are her four legged furry friends, music and traveling. She is an avid supporter and volunteer at Animal House Shelter animalhouseshelter.com in Huntley, Illinois. Contact Alexis at emailalexus10@gmail.com.

BE A FIREFLY

By Deborah Todd

I believe that in this lifetime I have been sent from the other side to bust the walls out of the status quo. I'm not a total insurgent, but challenging the container of uniformity seems to be my path. When I was five years old I learned my first lesson in conformity, or should I say lack of conformity. I, along with the rest of my kindergarten class was asked to color a hyacinth plant pink and in my childlike wisdom I decided that purple would be a happy color for my spring flowering bulb. My mother grew purple hyacinths and in my mind we could use some violet blooms in the classroom. To my disappointment and humiliation I learned that purple hyacinths were not acceptable or welcomed by my kindergarten teacher and I was dubbed a child that could not follow directions.

This challenge followed me along my childhood path as I bumped up against that familiar theme once again in elementary school. I was a musical child and from the age of seven was a zealous violinist in the school orchestra. Wanting to take on another instrument, I decided the following year that the percussion section would be a good place for me to strike up a creative beat. Did you know that in the 60's it was frowned upon to be a female and participate in the percussion section? After making my plea I was granted my percussion position, however I spent a lot of my concert band time playing the xylophone, cymbals, and the triangle; all female appropriate percussion instruments. You see it would not be fitting for a girl to pick up a set of drumsticks and tap out a street beat as she marched down the cobblestone parade route. I remember asking my dad if he would let me bring some bubble gum to drum class to share with my drum mates and music teacher. This was my way of easing and dealing with the uncomfortable feeling felt by everyone in the class, including me. I might add that this was also a time when girls were required to wear dresses to school. I just could not catch a break.

As I went through my school-age years, I began to realize that it was much easier to adapt by squelching my creative spirit and conforming. For years I had put a lid on myself to be what was considered appropriate. How can you stop a firefly from glowing? There is no light switch on a firefly, they just have to glow. Even though I continued to practice my lid approach, like a firefly, there were times when I just couldn't stop myself from glowing.

One of my favorite quotes is from Winston Churchill. who said, "We are all worms, but I do believe I am a glowworm."

I had one of the biggest eye-opening experiences during an intensive leadership class where simultaneously I was in the process of becoming a professional life coach. In this particular enlightening experiential exercise (and there were many), our personalities were typed in what was called an "I AM" exercise. In that enlightening exercise I learned that I was an "eccentric" personality type. The exercise happened to end right before we were to take a short break and I remember just sitting there in the classroom where I had just been dubbed an "eccentric". Stunned, motionless, planted in the seat like a lump, the pod leader came up to me after the rest of the class had dispersed, asking if I was all right after the surprising revelation. I gave some kind of appropriate response while all the time thinking to myself, "How did they all know that about me, I had worked so hard at keeping a lid on my creative expressive spirit?" In my defense, I feel the need to clarify the word "eccentric". In this exercise the definition of eccentric was not about being kooky, like I had originally thought. In this case it had to do with living out loud and in full creative expression. When I say our class was typed, it doesn't mean we weren't graced with other wonderful qualities. The identified types were just the primary points of power for each one of us, with the knowing that we were so much more.

What I had come to realize through that exercise was that by keeping a lid on my eccentric nature, I was not walking in my full power. In other words, I was not being my complete true self and therefore my full expression was on pilot light, and as a result I was actually robbing people of the gifts of my authentic nature. I had never thought of it that way before. My authentic nature, as well as yours, allows others to go to places they would never have gone before. I mean this metaphorically, of course. My pod leader shared with me that because of who I am, I give people permission to step outside of their box. It is like an extra shot of courage. I ask you, "When are you putting a lid on what you are passionate about?" "Are you being and doing what's always appropriate?"

These are great questions to ask. I had lived nearly half of my life choosing professions that took care of my survival, all the while being and doing things that did not quite light me up like a firefly. Every so often there were times when I would shake the status quo with the occasional spark and then shrink back in fear of not being accepted. More times than not I was compelled to keep that lid on, it was safer.

Last year I became a first time grandmother of identical twin granddaughters. Every day they remind me of how we come into this world without limitation. If they are unhappy, they express it. When they want something by golly they go and get it or scream until they do. I might add that we adults can sit with the two of them in a room for hours entranced with their every motion, watching them explore and discover new things. We are mesmerized with every gesture and expression of their being. Why is that? Are we recalling a time when we could do that too and now yearn for that opportunity to return to a life free of limitation? Do we want permission to fully express ourselves, to explore and go after what we want, just like a child?

There is such a mode of appropriateness surrounding our decisions. As adults, all that child-like magic has been taught right out of us. In my coaching work I am blessed to hear courageous stories about adults that have worked in careers that didn't keep them excited and then found themselves 20, 30 and 40 years later, gravitating to something that now brings them joy. Many of them had fallen prey to the chain of life and what that happy list holds. The formula: If you do this, then this and consequently do this, in this exact order you will have a wonderful life. I call this the "picket fence" condition.

I'm not judging the "picket fence" condition. However, I would encourage exploring what lights someone up early on. Making sure we have a balance of passion in all areas of life. As a coach I have an exercise I do with my clients called the "Wheel of Life". This wheel covers the eight primary areas of one's life. The client rates their level of satisfaction (1-10) in each of these eight categories; career, family and friends, significant other, health, money, personal growth, physical environment and last but not least, fun and recreation. Typically, fun and recreation are floating in the area of two or three. Remember our childhood, when we used to play and have a sense a freedom. It seems most of us aren't really doing the things that we love. Complete the self-directed coaching questions below to see how you're doing on the passion scale.

To complete the Wheel of Life Exercise, rate your feeling of satisfaction at this moment on a scale of 1 (low) -10 (High) for each area of your life listed below.

Career ___
Family and friends ___
Significant other ___
Health ___
Money ___
Personal growth ___
Physical environment ___
Fun and recreation ___

- Where in the above assessment would you like to passionately create a spark?
- Who do you have to be to fly like a firefly?

- What is one thing you are willing to change to be a glow-worm?
- Who will you tell?
- How will they know you've accomplished your change?

To tap into our own awareness, we have to look at where we are now and then decide where we are headed. Awareness is half of the equation. Be aware that when we want to change something, our personal saboteurs are sure to come out and play, having a way of sabotaging our success before we have even started. Make note of it and do it anyway.

Even though I felt uncomfortable being the only female in a male dominant percussion section, I did it anyway. I did not let that discomfort change my course. Sometimes we just have to push to the other side of the uncomfortable to gain confidence to walk in our passion, even if the world doesn't seem to agree.

Know that within you is a firefly waiting to cast the brightest, most vibrant light on all those around you, especially when you are flying. Walk in your authentic nature and know that you give others permission to walk along side of you, giving them courage to walk their own authentic path.

Go forth in GREATNESS and embrace with courage the passion of whatever is calling you.

About the author:

Deborah Todd, CPCC, PCC, is a highly interactive certified professional coach who has the ability to help people push away mind barriers that are stopping them from living their best lives and careers.

Along with Deborah's professional certifications with the Coaches Training Institute and ICF, Deborah is the first licensed Louise Hay Heal Your Life® teacher in Illinois, and has been described as energetic and passionate about empowering people.

MY CHALLENGE TO YOU

Thank for reading our stories!

I hope you found these stories inspiring, valuable and as energizing as I have. My co-authors energized me through their accounts and I am pleased to share these anthologies with you.

Now, it's your turn to *Seek Your Peak to* and perhaps chart a new course for your life. It is only when you share your passion with others that will you feel the real power inside you. You owe it to yourself to find your focus in life that will bring you fulfillment and satisfaction.

Spark your internal flame. Get glowing. Start now. Don't wait even a moment! Begin your journey to find and follow your passion.

Would you like to share your personal account of finding, following or living your passion? Join the conversation online at cyberlifetutors.com/seek-your-peak-to-find-your-spark-book/. Thanks again.

April M. Williams

REVIEWS

We Love Reviews!

Would you be willing to write a review of *Seek Your Peak to Find Your Spark* http://amzn.to/1eCmHOr on Amazon.com so I know if you liked these stories or not? I would really appreciate it.

April M. Williams

Other Works by April M. Williams

Seek Your Peak to Find Your Spark on Kindle http://amzn.to/1aIx7ky

Ignite Your Passion Kindle Your Internal Spark on Kindle amzn.to/18tqawQ

Ignite Your Passion Kindle Your Internal Spark in Paperback amzn.to/18tqtrB

Social Networking Throughout Your Career amzn.to/WirUX5

Networking For Results www.cyberlifetutors.com/store/

Press Pause Moments amzn.to/1bprxh0

www.ingramcontent.com/pod-product-compliance
Lightning Source LLC
Chambersburg PA
CBHW061652040426
42446CB00010B/1705